# Arise and Shine Forth

# Arise and Shine Forth

*Heeding the Call to Serve*

Jack Rushton Jr.

CFI
Springville, Utah

ISBN 13: 978-1-59955-118-0

Published by CFI, an imprint of Cedar Fort, Inc., 2373 W. 700 S., Springville, UT, 84663
Distributed by Cedar Fort, Inc., www.cedarfort.com

LIBRARY OF CONGRESS CATALOGING-IN-PUBLICATION DATA

Rushton, Jack L. (Jack Louis), 1938–
Arise and shine forth : heeding the call to serve / Jack L. Rushton, Jr.
p. cm.
ISBN 978-1-59955-118-0
1. Rushton, Jack L. (Jack Louis), 1938- 2. Mormons—United States—Biography. 3. Missionaries—Guatemala—Biography. 4. Missionaries—United States—Biography. I. Title.

BX8695.R87A3 2008
266'.93092—dc22
[B]

2008005278

Cover design by Jeremy Beal
Cover design © 2008 by Lyle Mortimer
Edited and typeset by Kimiko M. Hammari

Printed in the United States of America

10 9 8 7 6 5 4 3 2 1

Printed on acid-free paper

Dedicated to my father and mother, Jack Louis Rushton and Vera Bertell Young Rushton. My mom and dad instilled within my heart a love of The Church of Jesus Christ of Latter-day Saints at a very early age. Because of their goodness and willingness to do anything and everything to bless their children, I was able to serve a mission. They worked at night, after Dad got home from his work at Kennecott Copper Corporation, as custodians of the little school across the street from our home, to help finance my mission. They have long since passed on, but their influence lingers in the lives of their children and grandchildren. Though they themselves had little formal education, through their encouragement and teachings, their four sons all graduated from a university and went on to receive graduate degrees as well. My two older brothers were unable to serve missions because of World War II and the Korean War, but my younger brother and I benefited from a time of peace and were able to serve in the mission field. I am eternally indebted to my parents for everything good that I have done and accomplished in my lifetime. Enabling me to serve a full-time mission was their greatest gift to me.

# CONTENTS

# ACKNOWLEDGMENTS

I am indebted to my mother, Vera Young Rushton, for saving the majority of the letters I wrote home from Central America during the years 1958–61. They form the basis of this book.

My wife, Jo Anne, has given me constant encouragement and has been very helpful in the editing process. My son-in-law, Matthew Riley, has also been the source of good ideas in the editing process.

# PREFACE

I have felt impressed to write a book about my missionary experience in Central America from October 1958 to May 1961. My mission to Central America was the watershed event in my life. Without question, choosing to serve a mission was one of the most important decisions I have ever made. I want my posterity and friends to know what an impact it had on my life.

I have chosen the title for this book from D&C 115:5 in which the Lord commands that we arise and shine forth as we go to the nations of the earth to gather the precious souls of Heavenly Father to Zion. A call to serve a full-time mission among the people of Central America was the opportunity given to me as a young, unsophisticated, and untrained boy to literally "arise and shine forth" in bringing the message of salvation to a people who, in turn, blessed with the fulness of the gospel, would "arise and shine forth" and fulfill their destiny as sons and daughters of Abraham.

The Lord said in D&C 18:15, "And if it so be that you should labor all your days in crying repentance unto this people, and bring, save it be one soul unto me, how great shall be your joy with him in the kingdom of my Father!" I believe these words apply to me personally. I know for a fact that one of the souls I brought unto Christ as a result of crying repentance to the people of Central America was mine. How great is my joy as a result of my mission experience!

The personal impact of serving a mission was enormous in so many ways. Had I never served a mission, I would not have chosen a career teaching full-time for the Church Educational System. Perhaps I would not have been called to serve as a bishop, stake president, or patriarch. I doubt that I would have been able to deal with the accident that I experienced at age fifty without the spiritual strength I began to develop as a young missionary.

In the mission field I discovered the power of the word of God as contained in the scriptures. Beginning then and continuing throughout my life, the scriptures have truly been an "iron rod" connecting me to the love of God as manifested through His Beloved Son, Jesus Christ. The greatest desire of my heart is that my posterity will read this record of my missionary experiences and be inspired to accept their "call to serve" and that they will "arise and shine forth," reaping the same benefits and blessings that have been mine.

I am indebted to my mother, Vera Young Rushton, who kept all of the letters I sent home from Central America for the two and a half years I served my mission. These letters are the basis of this book. I have quoted extensively from them, and they have triggered memories that have helped me paint a more complete picture of my mission than I could have done otherwise. I have chosen to maintain the integrity of the letters by quoting them as I wrote them over forty years ago. However, I have made a few minor changes regarding the punctuation to make the letters more readable.

I wish I had had more wisdom in terms of keeping a more complete journal than I did. There are so many names of converts and fellow missionaries that have slipped from my mind over the years. My counsel to my posterity and to all those who go on a mission is to keep a detailed journal so that you can reflect back on all your experiences and have vivid recall of the work you did and how the Lord blessed you during that special period of time.

I have a firm testimony that our Heavenly Father loves His missionaries. Those who faithfully serve will be blessed not only during their years of service but throughout their lifetime. As I indicated, on my mission I began to build my life upon the rock of our Redeemer. In the years following my mission, I have continually searched the scriptures, made personal daily private prayer a priority, paid my tithing, kept the Sabbath day holy, tried to be clean in my thoughts and actions, and accepted every call to serve in the Church in whatever capacity. Through these years my faith in the Atonement of Christ has grown and developed. I have felt the enabling power of His Atonement in my life many times. Without this firm foundation established while serving a mission, I would have been ill prepared to deal with the adversity that later came into my life.

On August 1, 1989, shortly before my 51st birthday, I suffered a severe accident while body surfing at Laguna Beach, California. From that day to the present, I have been paralyzed from the neck down and living on life support. In retrospect, so many of the experiences I had as a young missionary helped to prepare me to deal with my paralyzed state. Although I was far from perfect, when the fateful day arrived and the storm literally broke upon my head with all its fury, I was not swept away into that "gulf of misery and endless wo" of which the scriptures speak because my life was built upon that "sure foundation—a foundation whereon if men build they cannot fall!" (Helaman 5:12).

May you who are young, especially my beloved grandchildren, read this record and be inspired and filled with a desire to share the message of the restored gospel to the people of this earth. As sons and daughters of Abraham through Ephraim, it is your foreordained mission to do so. Please apply the following scripture to yourselves all of your lives: "Therefore, thus saith the Lord unto you, with whom the priesthood hath continued through the lineage of your fathers—For ye are lawful heirs, according to the flesh, and have been hid from the world with Christ in God—Therefore your life and the priesthood have remained, and must needs remain in and through you and your lineage until the restoration of all things spoken by the mouths of all the holy prophets since the world began. Therefore, blessed are ye if ye continue in my goodness, a light unto the Gentiles, and through this priesthood, a savior unto my people Israel. The Lord hath said it. Amen" (D&C 86:8–11).

The establishment of the Church in Guatemala, and, subsequently, in all of Central America, was spearheaded by John Forres O'Donnal, whom I was fortunate enough to meet and work with while serving in Guatemala. As a recent graduate of the University of Arizona, he accepted a job with the United States government to move to Guatemala and plant an experimental farm—or plantation—to see if rubber trees could be cultivated in that climate. The United States was in the midst of World War II, and the production of rubber was a great concern at that time.

John O'Donnal lived in Guatemala for the rest of his life. He was anxious for the gospel to be brought to that land, and through his pleadings with the Brethren in Salt Lake City, missionaries eventually went to Guatemala. The following timeline of the growth of the Church in Guatemala was recorded in John O'Donnal's book, *Pioneer in Guatemala*. He is the ultimate expert regarding this timeline. As you examine the timeline, you will see that I arrived in Guatemala in November 1958. The first missionaries had arrived in Guatemala in 1947, and the first baptism—Carmen, the new Guatemalan wife of John O'Donnal—took place in 1948, just ten years before I entered the Central American Mission. At that time the Church was barely beginning to take root in the countries of Central America. In all of Central America, the only chapel built and owned by the Church was in Guatemala City. There were no wards or stakes, only branches and districts meeting in rented homes and buildings.

My estimates of the population of the cities and villages where I worked are probably not very accurate. These estimates were made through the eyes of a twenty-year-old North American, untrained and unschooled in making such estimates. I left Guatemala in 1961, about fifteen years before the great Guatemalan earthquake occurred on February 4, 1976. A number of the villages I worked in among the Mayan people—Patzicia, Patzun, and Tecpan—were nearly totally destroyed at that time. The government of Guatemala listed the destroyed populations of those villages in February of 1976 as follows: Patzicia, 7,100; Patzun, 8,300; and Tecpan, 5,900. Casualties and damages estimated by the government of Guatemala for the entire country included 22,368 dead, 76,415 injured, more than one million homeless, and 100 percent destruction of towns and villages in areas of greatest damage. Were I able to return to Guatemala, I wouldn't recognize most of the villages where I worked in the late fifties and early sixties.

The missionaries were the branch presidents and district presidents, and did much work with the auxiliary organizations. Our goal was to baptize men, confer the priesthood upon them, and train them to become leaders as quickly as possible. I was blessed to serve a mission in Central America when it was very much a pioneering effort. In the year 1959, my first full year as a missionary, there were only 300-plus baptisms in all of Central America. As you read this book and examine the timeline, you will see how, beginning in 1960 and continuing thereafter, the growth of the Church in Central America accelerated rapidly, almost unbelievably so.

The mission had not yet developed appropriate medical practices, and sickness was a very real and serious problem faced by most missionaries.

Yellow jaundice, parasites, and seemingly unending dysentery were some of the health problems many elders and sisters experienced serving during the late fifties and early sixties. Living conditions, for the most part, were very primitive and altogether it was a unique, challenging, and interesting time to serve a mission in Central America.

You will discover as you read this book that I was very critical of the Catholic Church. To the many good Catholic friends I have who may read this book, please know that my impressions of Catholicism in Latin America are those of a very zealous and young Mormon missionary. I loved the people of Central America, most of whom were Catholics. My impression of the organization of the Catholic Church in Central America was not favorable. If I were to return to Central America now, almost fifty years after my mission, perhaps my impression of Catholicism would be very different. What I say in this book is always about the organization and the hierarchy of the Catholic Church in Latin America and not the wonderful people I met and worked with.

When Elder Harold B. Lee, who eventually served as President of the Church from July 1972 through January 1974, and his wife came to the mission in 1960, he said that if somebody were to ask him whether he enjoyed his trip to Central America, he would say no. However, if they were to ask him if it had been an exciting, challenging, and spiritually rewarding experience, he would answer with an emphatic *yes*. That sums up my sentiments regarding the time period in which I was called to serve in the land of the Lamanites.

# TIMELINE OF THE CHURCH IN GUATEMALA

| | |
|---|---|
| May 21, 1942 | Arrival of John Forres O'Donnal in Guatemala |
| December 31, 1946 | John Forres O'Donnal visits President George Albert Smith, requesting that missionaries be sent to Guatemala |
| July 1947 | Central America made part of the Mexican Mission |
| September 4, 1947 | First missionaries arrive in Guatemala |
| September 7, 1947 | Dedication of Guatemala for the preaching of the gospel |
| November 13, 1948 | First baptism in Central America (Carmen O'Donnal) |
| June 12, 1950 | First branch organized in Guatemala City |
| August 22, 1950 | First property for construction of a chapel purchased by the Church in the name of John F. O'Donnal |
| November 16, 1952 | Central American Mission organized |
| November 16, 1952 | Dedication of Central America for the preaching of the gospel by Elder Spencer W. Kimball |
| January 8. 1953 | First full-time Lamanite missionary in Central America |
| 1953 | Coban, first Kekchi Indian area opened |
| January 9, 1955 | First chapel in Guatemala completed, dedicated by Elder LeGrand Richards |
| December 15, 1956 | First Cakchiquel Indian area opened |
| March 25, 1958 | Law prohibiting churches from owning property abolished; property for first chapel changed to name of the Church |
| *November 1958* | *Jack Rushton arrives in Guatemala* |
| February 21, 1960 | First Sunday School Board organized |

| | |
|---|---|
| July 5, 1960 | First Relief Society Board organized |
| *May 1961* | *Jack Rushton leaves Guatemala* |
| August 1, 1965 | Central American Mission divided; Guatemala-El Salvador mission created |
| June 29, 1966 | Church recognized by Guatemalan government and receives legal status |
| May 21, 1967 | First stake organized in Guatemala by Elder Marion G. Romney |
| 1967 | Seminary program started |
| 1975 | Cakchiquel Indians are first to have the gospel taught in their own tongue; teaching in Quiche, Kekchi, and Mam languages soon follows |
| October 25, 1975 | Quetzaltenango Guatemala Stake organized by Elder Bruce R. McConkie—first stake outside of Guatemala City |
| February 4, 1976 | Major earthquake in Guatemala |
| July 1, 1976 | Guatemala-El Salvador Mission divided, creating Guatemala Guatemala City Mission and El Salvador Mission |
| 1976 | Translation work begins in Indian languages |
| 1976 | Language training continues in Indian languages |
| February 21–22, 1977 | First Area Conference in Central America |
| June 27, 1977 | Latin Orientation Center (LOC) for Latin American missionaries initiated |
| July 1, 1977 | Guatemala Guatemala City Mission divided; Guatemala Quetzaltenango Mission created |
| 1978 | Construction of small chapels in rural areas of Guatemala |
| June 4–8, 1979 | First small chapels in rural areas dedicated by Elder Boyd K. Packer |
| June 10, 1979 | Reconstructed Patzicia chapel dedicated by Elder Boyd K. Packer |

| | |
|---|---|
| April 2, 1981 | Construction of Guatemala City Temple announced |
| September 12, 1982 | Groundbreaking for Guatemala City Temple |
| November 27–December 10, 1984 | Open house for Guatemala City Temple |
| December 14–16, 1984 | Dedication of Guatemala City Temple |
| December 1984 | Family History Center in Temple Annex |
| January 1985 | Missionary Training Center for Central America organized in Guatemala |
| January 1985 | Building for housing temple excursions leased |
| October 26, 1986 | Chimaltenango Guatemala Stake (first Cakchiquel Indian stake) organized by Elder Gene R. Cook |
| July 1, 1987 | Guatemala Guatemala City South Mission and Guatemala Guatemala City North Mission created |
| April 1990 | Carlos H. Amado (first Guatemalan General Authority) called to the Second Quorum of the Seventy |
| October 1, 1990 | Central America Area Office located in Guatemala; Area Presidencies called |
| October 19, 1991 | Guatemala dedicated by Elder Marvin J. Ashton |
| 1992 | Family history centers in stake centers; complete collection of Central America family history films obtained and housed in Temple Annex |
| January 1993 | Temple ceremony available in four major Indian languages (Cakchiquel, Quiche, Kekchi, and Mam) |
| July 1, 1993 | Guatemala Guatemala City Central Mission created |
| January 22, 1994 | MTC building in Guatemala dedicated; MTC president called |
| June 4–11, 1994 | Temple ordinances for Mayan kings performed in Guatemala City Temple |

CHAPTER 1

# *Snapshots from My Youth*

I believe the only way to fully appreciate the impact accepting a mission call had on my life is to see it in the context of my life's experience as a child and youth. Growing up where I did, very isolated from the world, without the soul-stretching and mind-expanding experience that resulted from my mission, it is difficult to say what my life may have been like.

A number of years ago, President Gordon B. Hinckley gave a talk about switch points and how they can affect our lives:

> Many years ago I worked in the head office of one of our railroads. One day I received a telephone call from my counterpart in Newark, New Jersey, who said that a passenger train had arrived without its baggage car. The patrons were angry.
>
> We discovered that the train had been properly made up in Oakland, California, and properly delivered to St. Louis, from which station it was to be carried to its destination on the east coast. But in the St. Louis yards, a thoughtless switchman had moved a piece of steel just three inches.

> That piece of steel was a switch point, and the car that should have been in Newark, New Jersey, was in New Orleans, Louisiana, thirteen hundred miles away.[1]

My mission was a switch point in my life. It put me on a track that led me to fulfill my foreordained mission in life. Without my mission experience, my life may have been far different from what it turned out to be. As a youth there were switch points as well that put me on the track that would ultimately enable me to accept the call to serve and reap the benefits.

I will share several snapshots of these metaphorical switch points from the photo album of my life that gave me faith to accept the call when it came and to successfully fulfill and complete my mission. It also should be evident from the snapshots what my life may have been like had I not accepted the call to serve.

**Snapshot 1: A testimony must be nurtured like a seed.** I was born in Ruth, Nevada, on September 26, 1938. My father, mother, two older brothers, and I lived in a little two-bedroom house on Grant's Hill. Ruth was a small mining town of roughly three thousand people and located about five miles from Ely. Ruth and Ely are about seven thousand feet in elevation and approximately 250 miles from Salt Lake City, Utah. Ruth was a company town, which meant that all of the families lived in company housing owned by Kennecott Copper Corporation Nevada Mines Division. Rent was fifteen dollars a month and most families did their grocery shopping at the Company Commissary, where they could charge their groceries against their next paycheck. We were a blue-collar, hardworking community that made a decent living but had little to no affluence.

In this little town we had a very small ward. I was the only boy my age active in the Church. I was never a Scout, never had a Young Men's program, and my mother was my only Primary and Sunday School teacher. I didn't realize it at the time, but she was an incredible teacher who had a firm testimony of the truthfulness of the gospel of Jesus Christ and a passion for sharing it. When I was in high school, we studied the Book of Mormon, and I received the highest score on the final exam. The prize was an autographed Book of Mormon from my mother. She was the one that helped me to feel that the Church was true.

**Snapshot 2: The gospel is true—even in Ruth, Nevada**. My dad was a less active member of the Church until I was about ten years old. While he may have been less active in the Church, he was never less active in the gospel. He was a kind man who had a multitude of friends because he sincerely loved others. His problem was smoking, which made him feel uncomfortable attending church. He had started smoking as a young boy while working with the ranch hands and cowboys his father had hired. They proved to be poor examples to young boys with regard to their language and living the Word of Wisdom. Mom was never sympathetic to his tobacco addiction, and I cannot ever remember seeing my dad smoke in the house or anywhere else for that matter. He wasn't proud of the habit.

When I was ten years old, he was sick with nephritis, a kidney infection, and was off work for a month. He had strict orders not to smoke or have any salt in his diet. One day while Mom was out of the house, he called me into the bedroom, gave me a five-dollar bill, and told me to go to the grocery store and buy him a carton of cigarettes and a bag of salted peanuts. As he handed me the money, I don't know what he saw in my face and eyes, but he took the five-dollar bill from me and said, "Oh h—, forget about it!" Soon after this experience he began to attend church.

On Sunday mornings my dad and I would go to priesthood meeting together at the American Legion Hall. After priesthood meeting we would go up the hill to the Serbian Hall, where we would hold Sunday School. The Serbian Hall was directly across the street from the Ruth Beer Garden. The Serbs were great beer drinkers, and when we would go to set up the hall for Sunday school there were beer bottles scattered all over the floor. As a deacon, it was always my responsibility to sweep the empty beer bottles into a back room, set up the benches, and help prepare the sacrament table. In the evening we would go to the old community church, which we rented for our sacrament meeting.

*Jack Rushton Sr. Family. Jack is the little boy in front with the striped shirt (circa 1945).*

During one sacrament meeting when I was twelve years old, as I was reclining on one of the benches, staring up at the ceiling and counting the holes in the acoustical tile, something the speaker said caught my attention, and I sat up straight and looked at him. He was a member of the high council, elderly, with white hair, and to my eyes he seemed to be older than Father Adam. He was bearing his testimony about Joseph Smith and the truthfulness of The Church of Jesus Christ of Latter-day Saints, and as he did so there came into my heart a warm feeling and into my mind the thought that this man knew that what he was saying was true. I can remember thinking that I too was glad to be a member of the true Church.

**Snapshot 3: Developing talents takes self-discipline.** In this little town tucked away up in the mountains of eastern Nevada, boys had only two things to occupy their leisure time: sports and music. We played baseball all summer long and then football in the fall, followed by basketball in the winter. I can't think of one boy my age who didn't participate in all three sports; it was simply our way of life. We also had in our little town a wonderful music program at our grade school. It was a very popular thing to play a musical instrument and to be part of the Ruth Grade School Band. In the fourth grade I started playing the clarinet and was taught the fundamentals of music by Ray Anderson, a carpenter for Kennecott Copper Corporation and also a great trumpet player and musician.

I loved music as much as I did sports, and when I was twelve I asked my mother if I could take piano lessons. We had an old upright piano in our living room that my mother would play from time to time, but none of us boys—my two older brothers and I—knew how to play. My mom said it was fine with her if I took lessons and if I was serious to go ask Mrs. Shartle, the town piano teacher, if she would teach me. Mrs. Shartle was a graduate of the Boston Conservatory of Music. What was she doing in Ruth? She had married a mining engineer who was hired by Kennecott to supervise the work in the mines, but he had suddenly passed away soon after their arrival in Nevada. Mrs. Shartle loved the town and the people and decided to stay in Ruth and support herself on her small pension and money from teaching piano lessons. I ran all the way to her house, which was perched high on a hill just across from the Star Pointer Mine. I knocked on her door, and she opened it and invited me in. I asked her if she would give me piano lessons. After learning who my parents were, she consented to teach me and had me sit down at her piano for my first lesson. She gave me several new books and an assignment to practice for the next week and sent me on my way. I was so elated I ran all the way home to show my mother the new books.

The next morning I arose early to practice the piano. I soon discovered that learning to play the piano was going to require a great deal of effort and work. Nevertheless, I practiced my lesson for the week and then ran outside to play baseball with my friends. The next day I was not quite as eager to practice, and after the fourth day I knew that this was something I did not want to have to do because it was apparently not going to be easy. I went to my mom and said, "Mom, I was just kidding. I really don't want to take piano lessons and learn how to play the piano."

She looked me in the eye and said, "Jack, did I ask you to take piano lessons?"

"No," I said.

She responded, "Now that you have begun, you are not going to quit!"

"But Mom," I said, "How long am I going to have to take lessons and practice the piano?"

She then spoke the most important word I would hear in my youth: "Forever!"

My fate was set. From that day until I left home to attend Brigham Young University at age seventeen, I practiced an hour each day on the clarinet and an hour on the piano. Although I was playing varsity baseball and basketball, my mother and I were committed to the proposition that I would practice my musical instruments each day. The practice would take place early in the morning and later in the evening when I returned from basketball or baseball practice. As time passed and my skills increased, I began to love the clarinet and the piano, and upon graduating from high school I received a music scholarship to Brigham Young University. Although I did not realize it at the time, developing the ability to play the piano would prove to be a great blessing on my mission.

**Snapshot 4: Overcoming personal obstacles prepares us for our life's mission.** I was born with an innate shyness to the point that it almost kept me from accepting a mission call when it came. I believe that most of us can relate to this personality trait. In a recent study I read that nearly 50 percent of adults in the United States identify themselves

as shy—experiencing discomfort or anxiety in some social situations, especially speaking in public. This was a problem I wrestled with through much of my life as a young boy and teenager.

The little Ruth Ward was the center of our lives as I was growing up. Until I was a teenager, we had no church building and met in various locations. When I was a young teenager, a wonderful thing happened to the ward that really didn't help me with my shyness problem but instead aided and abetted it.

When I was just beginning high school, the Ruth Ward was able to purchase an old abandoned hospital in Kimberly, a smaller mining town located just a few miles away. The hospital was brought to Ruth by a huge truck and placed on the basement dug by the men of our ward. The old hospital had one very large room used as the chapel. As I recall, there was also a small room at the back of the chapel that served as the bishop's office and another small room used as a classroom. I believe there was also a small kitchen. The remainder of the classrooms would eventually be in the basement. The bishop, Theo Anderson, hired me to be the custodian of our new church building, which I did throughout high school. Bishop Anderson took interest in me and was impressed that I could play the piano. He was one of the bosses for Kennecott and was probably the most affluent man in our ward. He found an old organ for sale and bought it himself and had it installed in the chapel. It was such an old organ that a deacon would have to stand behind it and turn a handle to pump the air through the organ so that it could be played. Later an electric motor was installed to take the place of deacon power.

I was the first organist that played this old organ for our Sunday meetings. I would practice all week to have the hymns prepared for Sunday. Bishop Anderson or one of his counselors would often call on me to play a piano solo in sacrament meeting as well. This was fine with me as long as I did not have to look at the congregation. I was extremely bashful and petrified at the thought of giving a talk in church. I believe the only talk I gave growing up was a two-and-a-half-minute talk in Sunday School when I was about nine or ten years old, and it was a disaster. I forgot what I was going to say. If you can imagine this, I stood before the members of our ward, twirling a hat on my finger with sweat streaming off my face, unable to remember one word that I was to speak. It really was a terrifying and humiliating experience for me. After that speaking disaster, I made it my goal to make sure it never happened again by not accepting any further speaking assignments.

All through my high school years, I never gave a talk in public but played many piano solos. I was so shy that I well remember the Christmas holiday I was home from BYU my freshman year and had accepted, against my better judgment, the assignment to speak in sacrament meeting in the Ruth Ward. I hate to admit it, but I feigned sickness that Sunday to avoid giving that talk. I had heard of people serving missions, and I knew that they had to talk in public and even knock on strangers' doors and talk to them about the gospel. I knew that I would never be able to do that and really put the thought of going on a mission out of my mind.

**Snapshot 5: Play the game of life hard, and play to win**. When I was fourteen, I played on a baseball team which included boys ages fourteen through eighteen. We won the state tournament, which was played in Reno that year, and defeated all the major powers from Reno and Las Vegas. As a result of winning the state championship, we earned the right to travel to Lodi, California, to represent the state of Nevada in the western regional tournament against California, Utah, and Arizona. Although we didn't win the championship, we did very well and had a wonderful experience. One great lesson I learned that year came from my dad. We had several practice games before going to Lodi for the regional tournament. Our coaches, in an attempt to keep us sharp, arranged for a team from Utah to go to White Pine County to play a double header with us. Knowing it did not really count, we didn't try very hard and were soundly defeated in both games. I especially didn't do very well. I struck out a number of times and made several errors in the field. I can remember thinking to myself that it was just practice and didn't matter all that much. This way I was able to salve my conscience.

After the games were over, my friends drove me home. As I got out of the car, I saw my dad standing in front of the house, waiting for me. He was a kind and gentle man, and we had a wonderful relationship. I always wanted my dad to be proud of me. In high school there were several times that I didn't do certain things with my friends because I knew that it would destroy the trust that he had in me. I was surprised to see him standing out in front of the house waiting for me. He said, "Jack, I'm disappointed in the way those games turned out today. I don't care if you win every game you play, but I expect you to give your best effort. When you put that uniform on, you are supposed to be a ball player. If you are not going to play the best you can, then don't put on the uniform." He put his arm around my shoulders, and we went into the house without saying any more. He had made his point, and I knew he was absolutely right. I felt bad, but I resolved then and there that I would never be guilty of not trying with all my heart in whatever I did. His advice would be invaluable when I eventually put on the uniform of a missionary and worked to serve with all my heart.

**Snapshot 6: We only have to decide once to do what is right.** As a new freshman in high school, I played the piano for three friends of mine who played a trumpet trio called Bugler's Holiday. We played all over the county at different locations and one Friday evening we were scheduled to play at the Elk's Club in Ely. That afternoon we went to practice and were left alone in the building. As we were leaving the building after our practice, one of my friends reached under the bar that was there and stole a bottle of whiskey. None of these friends were members of the Church, and they thought nothing of what they were doing. I was a freshman and wanted to make a good impression on these guys I went to high school with.

We got into the car and drove up into the hills outside of Ely. We found a secluded place to park, and the driver took the bottle, had a big drink, and then passed it to the guy sitting next to him. I was beginning to perspire heavily, wondering what I would do when the bottle got to me. Would I drink it? Would I throw it out the window? What could I possibly do to not be embarrassed? The bottle was passed from the driver to the person next to him. He also took a big drink and handed the bottle back to my friend sitting next to me in the back seat. I knew I didn't want to drink the whiskey, but I just didn't know what to do or what to say. My friend took a big drink and started to pass the bottle to me.

Just as he started to hand me the bottle, he looked at me and said, "Rushton, I'm not going to give you this whiskey. I know that you're a Mormon and wouldn't drink it. I'm not going to waste any of it on you." To this day I don't know what I would have done if the bottle had been placed in my hands. I gained a reputation that night that followed me through my high school years. Nobody ever asked me to drink, and I always had many friends who respected me and my standards. I have often wondered what my life would have been like if I had drunk the whiskey that night. I vowed then that I never wanted to be in a compromising circumstance without having first committed myself to the course of action I would employ, regardless of the situation. I learned that afternoon that you only have to make the decision once in your life to not smoke or drink.

**Snapshot 7: Perfect practice makes perfect.** I played varsity basketball my junior year in high school, but I developed a serious problem with my knees and the doctors told me that I couldn't play organized basketball that required me to practice every day. I was devastated because of the love I had for the sport, but it turned out to be a blessing in disguise. I turned all my attention to music and by the end of my senior year had been offered a music scholarship from BYU.

While at BYU as a freshman and sophomore, I was influenced by Professor Ralph Laycock, a man who had a profound impact on my life. He was the director of the concert band and was one of the finest musicians I have ever met. He played all of the wind instruments, but his favorite was the clarinet, and I made arrangements to take private lessons from him. I should mention that I was totally overwhelmed with BYU. I was considered to be an excellent clarinetist in Ely, Nevada, but at BYU I was faced with the bitter reality that out of twenty clarinetists in the concert band I was ranked fourth from the bottom. My self-esteem was at an all-time low when I finally had my first lesson with Ralph Laycock.

I went into his office one afternoon with some apprehension. He was a large man with bushy black eyebrows and piercing eyes. I had already observed him make returned missionaries shake in their boots during rehearsals because they were not performing the music the way they should. My knees were a little wobbly as I extracted my clarinet from its case. Professor Laycock asked me to play something, which I did, but after just two or three notes he grabbed the clarinet out of my hands and said, "Jack, you don't know how to play the clarinet!" I was mortified! He told me, however, that he thought I had some promise and that if I would follow his instructions and practice diligently, I might just learn how to play the clarinet.

He had me stand before a full-length mirror watching my hands to make sure they were holding the instrument correctly and also watching my mouth to ensure that the mouthpiece was properly inserted in my mouth. He took all of my music away and would only allow me to play whole notes while seeking to produce the pure and beautiful clarinet tone that, until I met Professor Laycock, I had been unable to do. Although it was extremely frustrating in the beginning, I followed his instructions and within a week or so I was exhilarated as I began to produce the beautiful, clear clarinet sound that had escaped me these many years. I found myself practicing six hours a day for Professor Laycock and made rapid progress. He helped me understand that only perfect practice makes perfect. He was the master teacher of the fundamentals of music and of playing the clarinet.

I persisted with my practicing, developing self-discipline, which only added to what my mother and Mrs. Shartle had instilled within me as a young boy. By the end of my sophomore year at BYU, I was second-chair clarinetist and was playing Mozart's "Concerto" for clarinet. I could never fully state how important the lessons I learned from music were as they enabled me to quickly learn Spanish and be an effective missionary.

### Note

1. Gordon B. Hinckley, "Watch the Switches in Your Life," *Ensign,* January 1973, 91.

CHAPTER 2

*Jack as a teenager with his father.*

# *Receiving the Call*

It was the summer of 1958. I was working for Kennecott Copper Corporation, Nevada Mines Division, in Ruth, Nevada. I had just completed my sophomore year of college at BYU, majoring in music. I was home that summer driving truck for Kennecott, saving money to finance my junior year at BYU. This had been the pattern during the previous two summers. I would make enough money during the summer working in the mines to finance an entire year of college without working part time. I was excited about my decision to become an accomplished musician and teacher. Although I did have a few friends who were leaving on missions, I had really never given it serious consideration because I thought it would hinder the accomplishment of my goal of being a serious musician, and I certainly could not envision myself speaking in public and knocking on strangers' doors.

The bishop of our ward in Ely, Nevada, Ward Gottfredson, called me into his office on one of my days off work. I had no idea what he had in mind, but I had great respect for him and was more than willing to keep the appointment. As he proceeded to issue me a call to serve a full-time mission, I went into a state of shock. Grasping for straws, I told him that if my patriarchal blessing indicated that I should serve a mission, I would go. He thought that was fine and told me to go home, read my blessing, and then come back to see him. My parents were out of town on a vacation, and I had no means of communicating to them the fact that the bishop had issued me a call to serve a mission. I ran into the house and, rummaging through my dresser, found the blessing buried beneath papers and books in the bottom drawer. Obviously, I had not read my blessing for years, having received it as a twelve-year-old.

I hastily opened the envelope containing the blessing and read each sentence more intently than I had ever read them before. I was relieved, actually, to finish the first page without discovering any reference to serving a full-time mission. Finally, however, as I neared the end of the blessing I read the words, "You will be a powerful emissary of the gospel among a people who are in darkness." It seemed to me that there was no question that it was the Lord's will that I was to serve a mission as part of my greater life's mission.

I sat there for a moment in my bedroom staring at the blessing, and then, because I had given my word to my bishop, I got back into my car and drove down to his office. I told him to begin the necessary paperwork and that I would like to leave as soon as possible. He was pleased, of course, but as I have thought about it many times since, I think he knew what I would find in my blessing.

Several days later, my folks returned from their vacation. As I heard the car drive into the driveway, I ran out to greet them. Before they could even get out of the car, I told them that I was going to serve a mission. They asked me when I wanted to go, and I told them as soon as possible. They agreed that would be just fine with them, and we began to talk finances. Things were different back in 1958. My mom and dad were the greatest people and strong members of the Church, but we just had never talked about my serving a mission. However, they were so happy that I was willing to go; they were and would continue to be very supportive of this important decision in my life. I should mention that my two older brothers, Allen and Darrel, did not have the opportunity of serving missions because the United States was at war when they were of missionary age. Allen served in the Navy during World War II, and Darrel was in the army during the Korean conflict. I was blessed to be of missionary age when the world was relatively at peace. My younger brother, Kim, was also able to serve a full-time mission in the Spanish-speaking San Antonio, Texas, mission.

Very quickly I had received all of the necessary interviews from the bishop and stake president, along with an interview from Elder Wirthlin, the presiding bishop of the Church, who had come to Ely to conduct a stake conference. (Interestingly enough, this Elder Wirthlin was the father of Apostle Joseph B. Wirthlin, who released me as stake president of the Irvine California Stake three months after my accident at Laguna Beach in 1989.) In those days an interview with a General Authority was part of the process of receiving a mission call.

All these things began to take place in July, as I recall, and in late August the call came from Salt Lake City. With trembling hands I opened the envelope and read the words that I had been called to serve in the Central American Mission headquartered in Guatemala City, Guatemala. The call was to be for two and a half years. My family and I had no idea where Central America was. We pulled out the encyclopedia and discovered that it was south of Mexico and north of South America. It might just as well have been on the moon for all we knew about it. We received information about what to bring, including a college-level Spanish grammar book of my choosing. In 1958 there was not a Missionary Training Center, so foreign speaking missions were two and a half years long because learning the language was part of the on-the-job training. Therefore, I was not blessed with a Missionary Training Center to attend prior to flying to Guatemala City. I was to report to the mission home in Salt Lake City in late October. That left me just about two months to continue working to save all the money I could and prepare to enter the mission field. I was so excited with the prospects of going to Central America that I had difficulty sleeping at night.

My job that summer with Kennecott Copper Corporation was driving truck in the large pit in Ruth. It is the deepest man-made hole in the world—a little over a mile deep. The operation in Ruth was a twenty-four-hours-a-day-seven-days-a-week business. They needed men for all that time and were willing to risk letting young college students drive those big trucks. Of course, they gave us the most undesirable shifts. I always seemed to be assigned the graveyard shift, which ran from 11:30 PM to 7:30 AM.

The trucks were monstrous. You had to climb up a short ladder to get into the cab, which always seemed to me like sitting on the roof of our house because I was so high above the road. These trucks had huge tires that were taller than I was. They had an automatic transmission, so all you had to do was either put it in reverse or drive and then press on the gas pedal. The power steering, however, worked well only when you were gunning the engine. This meant that as you descended into the pit, a mile straight down on a winding, narrow dirt road, every time you had to turn a hairpin curve, instead of applying the brakes you floored the gas pedal so you could steer better.

In the beginning it was very scary, especially because all of my driving was done at night. The Liberty Pit in Ruth was composed of multiple levels of varying widths that extended from the top of the pit to the bottom. On any given level enormous power shovels, much larger than the trucks we drove, would dig into the side of the pit where they were stationed and fill our trucks with dirt and rocks. They would take a massive bite into the side of the pit and almost fill the entire bed of our trucks with one shovelful. At the time, we were hauling waste to a dump outside of the pit a mile or so away. The dump was at least five hundred feet high, and we had to back up to the edge of it to empty our load. I can remember as though it were yesterday the fear I felt each time I backed up to the edge of the dump in a pitch-black night with my back-up light shining out into space. Several trucks that summer got too close to the edge and tumbled down into the dump. Fortunately, each time this happened, the drivers were miraculously able to jump out before their trucks went over the edge. After several weeks of work I became very confident in my ability to drive the truck and back up to the edge of the dump, which resulted in my becoming a little careless.

After I received my mission call, I somehow got the idea into my head that nothing could happen to me because the Lord had called me to serve a mission in Central America. I truly felt that I was invincible. For some reason I was working the day shift one morning when the shift boss drove up to my truck and told me to stop at the number 5 level and tell the cat skinner to bring his Caterpillar down to the bottom and clean up there. I had a full load on and anybody with any sense would have dumped their load and then stopped to talk to the cat skinner on the way back down. Anxious to obey my boss and in the ignorance of youth, on my way up out of the pit I turned off the main road to drive over to where the Caterpillar was working on the number 5 level.

As I turned off the main road the ground became very soft, and before I could even think about what was happening my truck began to tip over onto the driver's side. I was able to cling to the wheel until the truck had settled onto its side. It reminded me of a huge elephant trying to lie down. It tipped over so slowly that I was not injured in any way, but as it went down I had visions of my mission money flying away because of the accident. Standing on the driver's door, the cab was so wide I couldn't even reach the passenger door to open it. Within seconds men had crawled up onto the truck, opened the passenger door, and helped pull me out. As I stood dazed outside the truck, the boss drove up. I heard language from him that I had not heard before or since. I knew I would lose my job and the money that would help finance my mission, but to my surprise he just suspended me for five days to think about what I had done. Five days later when I went back to work I was a very humble and careful truck driver. I continued to drive truck until just a few days before I went to Salt Lake City and the mission home.

CHAPTER 3

# *The Mission Home*

Ely, Nevada, is only about 250 miles from Salt Lake City. During my life I had visited there many times. It was the nearest big city, and we always went to Salt Lake to treat serious medical problems or for any major shopping.

I was to enter the Mission Home in Salt Lake City the last week of October 1958. My dad had just undergone some minor surgery that could not be avoided prior to my departure. He wanted badly to drive me to the Mission Home, but instead I bid him farewell at the hospital before I left for Salt Lake City with my mom and older brother.

It was an emotional experience to say good-bye to my mom and other loved ones for two and a half years. I always suffered from homesickness when I was away from home. It had been a problem my first two years at BYU. Each time I would come home for a visit from BYU, the night before I left for Provo I would get so physically ill that I would throw up and be sick for several days. Thankfully my BYU experience helped prepare me to a certain extent for my two and a half years in the mission field. Even so, I have to admit that when all my loved ones had departed, I was lonesome despite being surrounded by hundreds of missionaries. I would learn that the cure for homesickness was hard work and the passage of time.

At BYU, I was allowed to take choir-conducting classes in place of the required religion classes because of my involvement in music. Although these classes would be very helpful in the mission field, I was not as familiar with the scriptures as I should and could have been. The only legitimate religion class I took was the mandatory Book of Mormon class. I did read the Book of Mormon, but my heart was not in it, and its impact on me was negligible. I had purchased a new set of scriptures for my mission. The pages had gold leaf on the edges, and because I had never opened them before I arrived at the Mission Home, the pages were all stuck together. I can remember turning my back to other missionaries or hiding in other ways as I tried to turn the pages of my stuck-together scriptures so they wouldn't know how inexperienced a gospel scholar I was. I was green! The only thing I had going for me was my faith that had caused me to accept a mission call in the first place.

The old Mission Home had been in use probably thirty or forty years for training full-time missionaries before their departure into the mission field. It occupied the place where the new Conference Center is now located. We were placed in large dormitory-type rooms and assigned companions who were going to the same mission. My companion turned out to be Joe Beecroft, a native of Provo, Utah. He had been pitching baseball at BYU and was a very good athlete. Because of my love for baseball, we had an instant rapport. He was tall and lanky and filled with self-confidence and enthusiasm. He was good for me because I was seriously lacking in self-confidence at the moment. We were only at the Mission Home for one week, and the time went by quickly. Due to my shyness, I was a little uneasy and very homesick, but the spirit of the mission president, his wife, the various teachers, the missionaries, and the many General Authorities who taught us that week helped me feel the Spirit. I began to realize what I had signed on to do, and I started to get excited. There was no systematic program for teaching the gospel at that time, but we were given many examples of how to teach about the Godhead, the Apostasy, and the Restoration. My head was just swimming with new ideas and, based on what I was learning, a conviction that The Church of Jesus Christ of Latter-day Saints was indeed true.

In 1958 we were not set apart for our missions by the stake president, as is done today, but by a General Authority at the Mission Home. I know I took it for granted then, but it is amazing to me now as I think about it that I was privileged to be set apart by Elder Sterling W. Sill, an assistant to the Quorum of the Twelve Apostles. Elder Sill was a great man who had written many books about leadership and was well known as an inspirational motivational speaker. I was intimidated in his presence but soon felt at ease as he placed his hands on my head and set me apart as a full-time missionary to serve in the Central American Mission. I wish I could recall the blessing he gave me, but I cannot. I do remember the good feeling that came to me as I realized that I was a missionary—an elder—set apart to preach the gospel to the people of Central America.

My most memorable experience in the Mission Home was the preparation I received to attend the temple for the first time and then my initial endowment session. In 1958 none of the missionaries were endowed before they went to Salt Lake City to the Mission Home. Since we were all to depart for our various fields of labor on Monday morning, we were scheduled to attend the temple for the first time the Saturday before our departure. The two days preceding our temple experience were spent listening to several General Authorities and others speak about the temple and its importance in our lives. At the end of those two days, I could hardly contain myself. I was filled with anticipation regarding the experience I was to have. I can remember that Friday evening looking out the window of our dormitory room at the angel Moroni glistening on top of the Salt Lake Temple. I didn't know what to expect exactly, but I knew that what would take place the next day would have a profound impact on my life forever.

At six the next morning, we walked across the darkened street to the temple. Being October 28, it was freezing outside, which made the warmth of the interior of the temple that much more noticeable to me. It wasn't just the physical warmth I felt, but it was as though I was enveloped with a spiritual warmth as well. I would not have been surprised to see angels. I was almost overwhelmed with the physical beauty of the temple and the astonishing workmanship of those early pioneer craftsmen. I didn't understand everything that took place during that endowment session, but I came away knowing that I had made sacred covenants with the Lord that would have an eternal effect. I felt warm, secure, and protected because of the garments that I would now wear for the remainder of my life. I didn't know what to expect in Guatemala, but my confidence and faith were bolstered by my temple experience and by the feeling of protection, both physical and spiritual, that came from wearing the sacred garments.

Although I was unprepared in so many ways for the cultural shock that awaited me when I arrived in Guatemala, my faith was strengthened by the Mission Home experience. That faith would carry me through those first difficult weeks and months in the mission field. I couldn't say the name of the church I represented in Spanish, nor did I know how to say the Book of Mormon in that beautiful language, but I did have a burning desire in my heart to learn to communicate quickly in order to teach those whom I had been called to serve.

# CHAPTER 4

# *Arrival in the Mission Field*

On Monday morning, October 30, 1958, eight of us—six elders and two sister missionaries—boarded a Pan Am propeller-driven airliner and flew to Los Angeles for a brief layover. As we were waiting in the terminal, Elder Cordell Anderson disembarked from an airliner coming in from Mexico City. He had just finished a two-and-a-half-year mission in Central America and was on his way home to Utah. His suit was worn out, he looked pale and tired, but he glowed with the Spirit. We gathered around him, and for the next hour he told us about Guatemala and the incredible experience he had had and that we would soon have in the land of the Lamanites. We were impressed by what he had to say and the way he said it. Elder Beecroft's older brother also came to the airport. He had served a Spanish-speaking mission in Mexico, I believe. His message to us was to learn to speak Spanish as well as possible. He told us that our command of the Spanish language would endear us to the people and entice them to listen to our message. As I look back over my mission experience, I believe that what he said was true. I took to heart his counsel and set as one of my goals, right then and there, to learn the Spanish language to the best of my ability. Meeting those two elders at the airport helped increase my excitement about being a missionary in Central America. I could hardly wait!

Later that day we boarded another Pan Am airliner and flew through the late afternoon and evening to Mexico City, where we would have a three-day layover. This layover would prove to be a great aggravation to our mission president, Ernest L. Wagner. We were housed in a beautiful hotel in downtown Mexico City. The food was wonderful, and I was beginning to think that this mission was great. The Murdock Travel Agency that made all of the travel arrangements for the missionaries had arranged several tours for us during the time we would be in Mexico City. We visited Chapultepec Park and the Paseo de la Reforma, which is at the heart of downtown Mexico City. It was beautiful and fascinating, but the thing I will always remember the most is the visit we paid to the pyramids outside of town.

As we viewed the pyramids, all we could think of was the Book of Mormon, the Lamanites, and that we were viewing the remains of their ancient civilization. We were beginning to feel something that would be much stronger in Guatemala: we were indeed walking where Nephi, Alma, Mormon, Moroni, and all the other great Book of Mormon prophets had walked and prophesied of the coming of the Savior to this promised land. Would we in fact walk where Christ had walked when He appeared to the people on this continent so many centuries before?

After three fascinating days, we again boarded a Pan Am flight to Guatemala City. It didn't seem like a long flight, and about noon we landed at the international airport in Guatemala City. As we walked out of the airplane and down the ramp, it felt as if we had entered a steam bath. The heat and humidity were incredible, and its effect was intensified for me personally as I had grown up in Ruth, Nevada, which was seven thousand feet in elevation. The air where I grew up was either warm and dry or very cold and dry. This was only the beginning of the many cultural shocks I would encounter in the next few days. President Wagner and his assistants were there to greet us as we disembarked. We received a warm greeting, but he was visibly upset and wanted to know where we had been. We described our visit to Mexico City, and he became more unhappy, not with us but with the Murdock Travel Agency. Although I don't know for sure, I imagine that a phone call was made to Salt Lake City that day by an unhappy mission president. We were the only group to have such an experience in Mexico City.

It was my privilege to ride in the back of the big mission Buick from the airport to the mission home. As I look back on it, I think President Wagner intentionally drove us through the most poverty-stricken part of Guatemala City to the mission home. I could not believe what I was seeing as we sped through the streets. There were open sewers in many of the streets, and the scent was less than sweet. Raggedy-looking brown people were walking all over, some selling their wares at the side of the street and others buying. It was an incredible cultural shock for me. I had never been exposed to this kind of poverty. Our tour guides in Mexico City, I discovered, must have kept us in the best part of town. We certainly didn't see any other Buicks on the streets from the airport to the mission home.

The mission home looked beautiful to me, and coming from Ruth, Nevada, I thought it was better than any house in our town. Sister Wagner greeted us, and we were soon sitting down to a carefully prepared dinner in a beautiful dining room. I was thinking that this mission was getting better and better each passing day. President and Sister Wagner were very formal people and were not prone to public expressions of warmth and affection. However, I felt their goodness and had great respect for both of them. President Wagner always reminded me of a Marine drill instructor. He was disciplined and expected us to follow his example. We visited into the evening and then they told us our new assignments. I was the last to receive my assignment and was told I would have the privilege of working in the Indian village of Totonicapan. There was no way I could even pronounce the name of the town I was being assigned to, and I began to feel a little uneasy when the president revealed to me that I would be traveling from Guatemala City to Totonicapan by myself. It would take most of the day, but he assured me that I should arrive well before the sun went down.

I had difficulty sleeping that night, as did most of my fellow missionaries with whom I had traveled to Central America. I tossed and turned and wondered what tomorrow might bring. I had no idea. Early in the morning President Wagner took me in the mission Buick to a large bus terminal. The buses were not luxury liners like I had seen in the United States but were old school buses painted myriad colors with different titles in Spanish painted on their sides. Of course, at that time, I had no idea what these Spanish words meant. We bypassed all the buses and ended up at a row of old beat-up station wagons. They were called "carros rapidos."

They stuffed two people up by the driver and four more in the back seat. President Wagner told the driver to take me all the way to Quezaltenango and that there would be people to meet me. I didn't realize that Totonicapan was beyond Quezaltenango on a road that would wind up into the mountains to that little village. The president told me the instructions he had given to the driver, gave me an embrace, and away we went. I was sandwiched between three Guatemaltecos in the back seat and was scared to death. Where I came from, Hispanics did not have a good reputation, and I think most people in my community were a little racially prejudiced.

I was afraid to go to sleep, thinking that maybe I would be knifed and have my money and suitcases stolen. I tried to enjoy the beautiful countryside but found it very difficult to concentrate on anything other than self-preservation. After several hours on the road, we pulled up to a public square in a little town. I needed to use the bathroom and was getting thirsty, but I was afraid to leave the carro rapido, thinking that I might get left behind. All of a sudden two Mormon missionaries, easily recognizable because of their white skin, suits, and hats, happened to be walking through the public square, saw me, and stopped to say hello. They knew how green I was and could sense my uneasiness, so they were very kind to me and assured me that I would soon be in Quezaltenango.

Toward evening we arrived in Quezaltenango. I later would learn that it was quite a large city, but I was so dazed and exhausted that I couldn't quite take it all in. Thankfully, my new companion was there to meet me, along with some other elders from Quezaltenango. I can remember the sense of relief that flooded my system upon seeing these missionaries. Most of the other people that I could see were native Mayan Indians colorfully dressed in a manner I had never seen before. My companion was Elder Haws, a short, wiry, and enthusiastic young man. He was just finishing the last month of his mission, and I would soon learn that he was determined to work as hard as he could until the day he boarded the airplane to return to the United States.

Our bus was just leaving for Totonicapan, so we didn't have any time to visit just then. Running as fast as we could with my bags in our hands, we climbed aboard the bus just as it was pulling away from the bus terminal in Quezaltenango. The bus was an old school bus like I had seen in Guatemala City. Because the Mayan Indians are so short, the seats had been placed closer together than in a normal bus in the United States. The bus was packed with Guatemalan Indians, or "Naturales" (the worst insult you could give to anybody was to call him an Indian). I am not very tall—five feet three inches—but my knees were tucked up under my chin, and I was very uncomfortable. There were chickens and pigs riding in the bus with us, and the odors that permeated the atmosphere were incredible. I smelled things I had never smelled before. I felt that my companion and I were probably the only two people on the bus who had ever had a bath. As I sat next to my companion for the next several hours, however, I thought maybe only I had bathed recently.

# CHAPTER 5

# *Totonicapan*

From Quezaltenango we kept going higher and higher into the mountains, finally leaving the paved highway and going forward on a rough dirt road. By now it was dark, and not being able to see anything out the window was scary. I began to think that we were going to the end of the world, but finally I could see some scattered lights ahead on the mountainside, and my companion informed me that we were entering the outskirts of Totonicapan. We came into town on a narrow cobblestone street and stopped in the public square. The square was quite large with a big fountain in the middle. There was a huge Catholic cathedral on one side, public buildings on the other side, and various shops composing the rest of the square. We retrieved my bags from the top of the bus, and without a word Elder Haws began walking rapidly down the cobblestone street. I followed behind him through the dark street. In all of Latin America the homes are built on the street with no front yards. You go through a large door that in most cases lets you into a patio area, which is surrounded by the remainder of the home. We hadn't walked far before we came to what would be my home for the next four months. Elder Haws opened the door that was right on the street, and we entered a patio area with a *pila* (fountain) in the center. It was very dark by now, and it was difficult to see what our home was like. Elder Haws had told me that our residence was also the chapel for the branch.

Because of how late it was, we went directly to the bedroom. The room was totally enclosed and had no windows. A single light bulb dangled from a cord from the ceiling, barely illuminating the room. The beds were old

*Elder Rushton and the maid's three children.*

and rickety, and along with a couple of old beat-up chairs and a table, this constituted the extent of our furniture. Talk about a contrast between Mexico City, the Mission Home, and now Totonicapan. It was very cold, and the only heat we had was a little electric space heater that you couldn't feel unless you were sitting on top of it. I learned later that Totonicapan was probably the coldest town in the mission. For most of the time I was there, I would wear my pajamas under my suit with a sweater on top and then a heavy overcoat. I was still cold. The humidity was high, and the cold penetrated clear to the bone.

I unpacked and was soon in bed trying to sleep. I kept hearing through the night the cheeping of what I thought were birds, but I could not figure out how I could hear birds with no windows in the room.

After a very restless night, my companion had me up at about 5 AM. I asked him what the cheeping was, and he informed me that large rats lived in the walls of our bedroom. He then showed me a little hole in the wall covered by a tiny door with hinges on it. The elders, always ingenious, would put poisoned tortillas into the wall periodically, and the rats would eat them, get terribly thirsty, and run out onto the patio and die.

About that time I wasn't feeling well, but in that dimly lit, cold room I had my first spiritual experience in Guatemala. Elder Haws had me stand up, and facing each other we sang the hymn "The Morning Breaks" by Parley P. Pratt. We sang it in Spanish, and from that point on it became one of my favorite hymns while in the mission field and since.

We knelt in prayer and then had a study class together. Elder Haws gave me some good advice regarding my study of Spanish. He told me that if I would use as many of my senses as I could that I would learn the language much more quickly. He gave me a piece of paper, and I began to learn how to conjugate the verbs. I would write the verbs with their appropriate conjugation and pronounce out loud what I was writing. Using this system, I was using my eyes, my voice, and my ears. He also had me take my English copy of the Book of Mormon and lay it side-by-side with my Spanish copy. I would read out loud from the Spanish copy and then read the same verse in English to understand what the Spanish meant. The time went by quickly that morning, and soon it was time for me to be introduced to our kitchen.

The best way I can describe our kitchen is that it looked like the black hole of Calcutta. I was surprised and happy to learn that we had a full-time maid. For fifteen dollars a month from each elder, we were able to hire a maid who would come early in the morning, cook all our meals, make our beds, wash our clothes, and do the daily shopping at the marketplace. We did not have a refrigerator, so daily shopping was a necessity. Our maid was a sweet woman who brought her two little girls to work with her each day. I can't remember very well what we ate that first morning, but I remember that we stirred powdered milk into boiling water. I thought it strange at the time but came to realize that drinking the water in any of the villages without boiling it would always bring sickness in the form of dysentery. In all the time I worked with the Indians, I never took a drink of water but drank a lot of sodas and hot milk. We would boil water and then stir in a special brand of powdered milk that I believe was manufactured in Mexico. This was always our breakfast drink in Totonicapan. That morning I was introduced to sweet bread, which was very good. It was purchased hot each morning from the local bakery, and it stands out in my mind as one of the real edible things I had the first few days I was in Totonicapan.

My first week in Totonicapan, Elder Haws and I left about 4:30 PM and took a two-and a-half-hour walk into the countryside to a place called Pa Qui. We left so late in the afternoon because the Indian men worked in the fields until dark and none of the women spoke Spanish. We tried to arrive there just as it was getting dark. The walk to Pa Qui was one of the most beautiful I had ever taken. Before my mission whenever I had thought of Guatemala, I had thought of a big jungle. I was surprised to learn that high in the mountains, where I was, it was a forest of evergreen trees. They looked like ponderosa pines. As we walked on the dirt road, we did not see any kind of vehicle. We passed a few Indians walking toward Totonicapan, and they smiled and greeted us. We must have been a strange

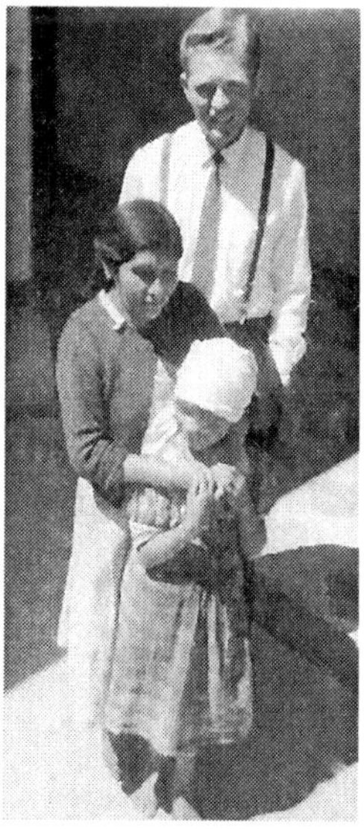

*Elder Rushton with the maid and her daughter.*

sight to these people. Here we were dressed in full suits, white shirts and ties, and *hats.* To me it seemed strange to wear a hat every day, but it was a mission rule. My first hat was black, small brimmed, and very stylish for the day. A Guatemala City newspaper advertised a hat that looked a great deal like mine as *Estilo Mormon* (Mormon style). Just as missionaries today are recognized by the white shirt and tie, we were recognized by the hats we wore. The fact alone that we were *gringos* would have brought us great attention, but to be dressed as we were, it would be a great understatement to say that we stood out.

At about 7 PM we arrived at the village, which consisted of adobe huts with thatched roofs. These little homes had only one room with a dirt floor and a fire pit in the middle with no way for the smoke to get out except through the door. The only furniture was a couple of beds along the sides of the room. There were roosters in the rafters and pigs under the beds. Talk about a cultural shock! Pa Qui was a very tiny village with no commercial establishments. It was just a cluster of small adobe homes surrounded by fields in which the Indians worked. However, twelve members of the Church lived there, and the elders made a point of visiting the village several times each month.

The word went out that the missionaries had come, and soon about fifteen men, women, and children had gathered together in a member's one-room adobe home to hold a meeting. We sat on the beds and the floor with the only light coming from the fire that had been kindled in the little fire pit in the center of the floor. It reminded me of holding a meeting out in the woods while gathered around a campfire. Most of the people only spoke their Indian dialect, and the Spanish they did speak was not very good. Because of my own bad Spanish, I related to these beautiful, humble Lamanite people. It was an informal meeting similar to a testimony meeting. Elder Haws spoke, as did most of the men who had gathered together. After about an hour, everyone seemed to have spoken all they wanted to, and we began to sing the hymns together. As we sang, the roosters began to crow. What an experience! These

*Elder Rushton and members in Pa Qui.*

people loved to sing, and we sang hymn after hymn together in that little adobe hut. I felt a great spirit that night with those people.

It was almost 10 PM when we started our two-and-a-half-hour walk back to Totonicapan. Although it was late at night, we had no trouble walking on the road because of the brightness of the moon. It was a full moon, and it seemed that I could reach up and touch it because we were so close to the equator. I felt I was truly in Book of Mormon country and could somehow feel the presence of the Book of Mormon prophets about me. The last mile or so was uphill, and when we reached the chapel-home, it felt good to finally lie down and go to sleep.

Elder Haws either had a great work ethic or was really trying to impress me. My first full week in Totonicapan we taught seventy discussions. In those days we called them cottage meetings, and that was one of the items that we reported on our weekly report to the mission president. It was the most discussions my companion had ever given in one week during his entire mission. We were working fourteen hours a day, which was also an item we included in the weekly report to the mission president. We were getting up at 5 AM, studying until 6:30, and then hitting the street to go tracting or fulfilling appointments we had previously made. We were up and out so early in the morning to catch the Indian men before they left to work in the fields. The majority of the women could not speak Spanish, and it was inappropriate to visit with them without their husbands at home. After trying to visit a few families, we generally would come home about 9 AM to eat a little breakfast and study for a period of time. I admit that I did not contribute much to the missionary discussions at this early stage. I couldn't speak Spanish and could not understand what was being said. Every time I would doze off during a discussion, my companion would kick me in such a way that the investigators wouldn't see him do it. I hate to say it, but during those first few weeks he had to kick me quite a few times. From the beginning, however, I loved those Indian people. They were humble, and although I couldn't understand what was being said, I felt a good spirit around them.

My first week in Totonicapan was what I call the honeymoon of my mission in Guatemala. Shortly after that, I got very sick with dysentery that just would not go away. With the dysentery came terrible homesickness and depression. I could not believe that it was possible for me to spend the next two and a half years living under those conditions. One night while I was trying to sleep, I got very sick and made a mad dash for the bathroom, which was on the other side of the patio from our bedroom. It was not a beautiful bathroom, but thankfully it did contain a sink and a flush toilet. As I was running, I had forgotten that there was a clothesline stretched across the patio, and it caught me around the neck and threw me to the tile floor on my back. Needless to say, I did not make it to the bathroom!

As I lay there on my back, sick and hurting, looking up at that inky black Guatemala sky full of stars, I cried out, "If my dad could only see me now and know how I am living and how sick I am, he would send me an airplane ticket so that I could go home. He would never permit one of his sons to live this way and suffer so much." As I lay there, the thought came to me that my earthly father could not hear me or help me, nor could anybody else in Totonicapan. And so I rolled over onto my hands and knees and for the first time in my life—from the depth of my soul—I pleaded with my Heavenly Father for His help. I had prayed before, but I had never been placed under circumstances in which the only available help was from God. I just had to have help, and He was the only source from which it could come. I did not see an angel or hear an audible voice that night, but the Holy Ghost descended upon me as I had never experienced it before. I was filled with warmth, peace, and comfort to such an extent that I knew in my heart that not only could I endure two and a half years in this land but that I would also come to enjoy it and love the people. The young missionary that got out of bed the next morning was a far different person from the one that had gone to bed the night before. I still struggled with homesickness for several more months, but I was comforted that the Lord would help me through any difficulty I might encounter.

The lesson I learned that night about prayer has sustained me throughout the remainder of my life. My accident on August 1, 1989, was a devastating experience. My spirit had difficulty accepting what had happened to my body. It just seemed that I had lost so much—the use of my physical body and my career with the Church Educational System. I thought I had also lost my ability to serve in the Church. How could I ever be an effective husband and father in this condition? I wasn't bitter toward God, nor did I go around saying, "Why me?" However, I did not know how long I could live being paralyzed from the neck down and on life support. At this time the Lord inspired me to approach Him with intense fasting and prayer, which I did. In doing so, I had an experience even more powerful than the one I had in Totonicapan that night so many years ago. It was through mighty prayer and fasting that the Lord healed my soul and gave me heart. Despair was replaced with joy, peace of mind, and a sense of well-being that has continued with me through the intervening years. Through heartfelt soul-searching and sincere prayer, I have been strengthened to be able to deal with all the challenges that I have faced during my lifetime. Without my Totonicapan prayer experience as a young missionary, I don't believe I would have had the faith in the efficacy of prayer to deal with the challenges of life and particularly my paralysis.

Totonicapan was quite a large town. With all the outlying areas, there may have been as many as ten thousand people living there. I was impressed with how self-sufficient this town seemed to be. There were shoemakers, tailors, saddle makers, hat makers, and weavers. Almost every other house on the main streets contained a little store. To me it was a quaint and interesting place. In Totonicapan I was introduced to my first marimba band. Totonicapan had its own band of four men paid by the government just to provide music in the town. They played day and night, and whenever I hear a marimba band playing, my mind immediately goes back to that little Indian town in the mountains of Guatemala. Also, regardless of how dilapidated a home may have been, it was not uncommon to see a beautiful radio sitting in a prominent place. Emanating from these radios was a constant concert of marimba and Mexican mariachi music.

I had just completed my first month as a missionary when Elder Haws was transferred to Quezaltenango to complete the last few weeks of his mission. My new senior companion was Elder Wilson from Colorado. Elder Wilson was a little older than the average missionary. He had been married for about a year when his wife was killed in a car accident. Having no children, he had a great desire to serve a mission. His father, a wealthy nonmember, told him that if he left on a mission he would be disinherited. Elder Wilson heeded the call of the prophet and was in the last three or four months of his mission when he was assigned as my companion. His father did not write him a single letter the entire time he was gone from home.

Elder Wilson had red hair, was fairly large, and related well to the Indian people. He was a more effective missionary than Elder Haws in terms of communicating with the people. His drawback, however, was that he was always sick and did not work the long hours Elder Haws did. To this day I do not know if his sicknesses were psychological or really physical, and I don't think he knew either. Based on the time we spent together, I would say he was a very good person. Anyway, many were the days that I spent studying while he was asleep in bed. Regardless of his condition, I would get up at 5 AM and spend the entire day studying Spanish and the scriptures. I was consumed with a desire to learn Spanish and the gospel. I would bundle up in my pajamas, my suit on top of them, a sweater, and a heavy wool overcoat. I would turn up the old electric space heater to its highest level and then sit as close to it as I could. Then I would study until midmorning when the sun would shine into our patio. I would then go out and find a sunny place in which to sit and continue my studies.

At this early time in my mission, I was reaping the rewards of having learned self-discipline from my mother, my piano teacher, Mrs. Shartle, and Professor Ralph Laycock. I was able to get out of bed early and study for hours at a time, which was a blessing to me in learning the gospel and Spanish. The discipline I gained from long hours of practice on my musical instruments blessed me both as a missionary and throughout my life.

I discovered that one of the best ways to learn vocabulary was to try to talk to the young children in the branch. I would point to some item like my tie or shoes and then ask them how to say it in Spanish. They would tell me, and I would immediately forget, and they would just bust up with laughter. They were always willing to help me, however, and I began to love the little children of Guatemala. We had an old piano in our chapel-home, and I played for sacrament meeting, Sunday School, Primary, Priesthood meeting, and Relief Society. I think my ability to play the piano helped me relate to the people, who had such a love for music.

During that time period I met a man who had a profound influence on my life, then and now. His name was Juan Mejia. He was in his late fifties when I met him at the branch in Totonicapan. His wife had passed away, and he was living alone in a little adobe hut in the mountains. During the day he worked as a weaver, which was the common profession among many of the people in the mountains of Guatemala. They wove blankets and beautiful cloth, or *tela*, as they called it. He earned a meager wage that barely provided him with the necessities of life. His clothes were raggedy, and his sandals were made of discarded rubber tires.

Each Sunday he would walk down the mountain to the chapel and spend the entire day with us. We put our garbage in a fifty-gallon drum, which he would strap to his back and carry out to the dump outside of town. His pay for his work was to eat with us at lunchtime between meetings. The menu was always pretty much the same—beans, rice, and corn tortillas. We would dish him up a huge plate of beans, which he would consume in just a few seconds. We would ask him if he would like more beans, and he would smile and say yes. He would always eat at least four huge servings of beans each time he ate with us. In my innocence I asked my companion why Juan could eat so many beans. My companion informed me that Juan was so poor that he could not afford to buy beans and that his daily diet consisted basically of corn tortillas. Eating lunch with us each Sunday was the highlight of his weekly life as far as food was concerned.

He would go with us from time to time to visit the members of the branch. Whenever we entered a home we would have a prayer, and the member offering the prayer would say something to the effect that "we are happy to have the missionaries here and are honored with the presence of Brother Juan Mejia." Brother Mejia was a spiritual giant. He diligently searched the scriptures each day. During his lunch hour, he would sit under a tree and read the Book of Mormon and eat a banana. His knowledge was profound, and all the members of the branch realized that he probably knew more than the missionaries. As I began to understand this, I was humbled. Here I was, a member of the Church all of my life with all of the advantages of education and living in the United States of America, and this little Guatemalan Indian knew much more about the gospel of Jesus Christ than I did. I resolved then that if the Lord would permit me to live long enough, I would devote myself to scripture and gospel study to at least know as much as Brother Juan Mejia. Through the years I have pictured him with our garbage can on his back, walking in his raggedy clothes and rubber-tire sandals through the dusty streets of Totonicapan to the garbage dump. Who would ever know from his looks what was in his heart and in his mind with regard to the saving truths of the gospel of Jesus Christ? When I am tempted to be slack in my reading of the scriptures, the vision of this man is a compelling reminder of my commitment to gospel study.

*Elder Rushton, Juan Mejia, and Elder Wilson.*

The scriptures have been such a vital and important part of my life. I must pay tribute to Juan Mejia for being the initial inspiration that started me on the road to in-depth scripture study. As I was lying in the intensive-care unit in a trauma center a few days after my accident in 1989, unable to breathe, move any part of my body, or speak, a good friend of mine, Ron Wilson, created a chart through which I was able to communicate my needs. It was so well thought out and put together that I could indicate by blinking my eyes, not only what my physical and emotional needs were, but also what book, chapter, and verse of scripture I wanted read to me. Good friends from my high priest group as well as members from our high council took turns sitting with me through the long nights so that my wife, Jo Anne, could go home, be with our little girls, and get some rest. Because of a lifetime spent searching the scriptures and following the example of Juan Mejia, I was able to have these wonderful friends read my favorite passages of scripture over and over again all through the night. I was comforted as the powerful words of the Lord contained in the scriptures brought hope and peace to my soul. Since that time I have had voice recognition software installed on my computer that makes it possible for me to continue to search the scriptures. They still bring me the strength, hope, and the peace I need to go forward with my life. I believe I know why the rod of iron in Lehi's dream symbolizes the word of God. The scriptures have truly been like an iron rod connecting me to the love of God, which I have firmly clung to, not with my hands but with my mind and spirit. It has made all the difference in my life. I am so blessed to have met Juan Mejia as a young missionary.

As Christmas approached, we began to prepare a special program to be held on Christmas Eve for the branch. We recruited all of the children in the branch and began to train them for the typical Christmas pageant. They were so excited to participate in this little program. Even though I had been in Totonicapan just a short time, I loved the little Indian children. None of them had shoes, and for the most part they all dressed like Juan Mejia. They were humble and sweet and appreciative of any little thing you did for them. This was the first Christmas I had done anything for anybody else by way of service. My heart was full of the Christmas spirit—the spirit of Christ.

Elder Wilson and I made all of the scenery for the pageant. I was the sound effects man as well as the designer of costumes, which were all made of crepe paper. Elder Wilson and I went to the market and bought 150 oranges for $2.50 plus a big stalk of bananas. We also bought ten pounds of candy for Santa Claus to give away on Christmas Eve. The anticipation of the children for this great event hung heavy in the air. Finally the great day arrived, and the program and Christmas Eve celebration were a great success. We were able to dress Elder Wilson up and successfully pass him off as Santa Claus. The members of the branch prepared tamales wrapped in banana leaves and cooked them in boiling water in a fifty-gallon drum. At midnight fireworks were set off, and I truly realized that this was not Christmas in the United States. Beginning a week or so before Christmas, all the people would cover the floors of their homes with fresh pine needles. The smell was wonderful and turned the most humble home, at least for a month, into something festive and special.

As the weeks went by, my testimony of the work began to grow and deepen. I was beginning to understand some fundamental truths about missionary work. In a letter from Totonicapan dated January 6, 1959, I wrote the following to my parents:

> The thing we strive for in missionary work is to preach and teach by the spirit of the Holy Ghost. Without it you might as well be home. I have often heard people say that this Church probably wasn't true because none of the preachers have ever been to college to learn the doctrine, etc., but the truth of the matter is that a baby can teach the truth. This gospel of ours is so simple it's hard for people to believe it. People are always looking for some black magic and sorcery, but they won't find them in the Church of Christ. Because the gospel is life itself—Where did we come from? Why are we here? Where are we going? How do we get there? This is the gospel. There's nothing else and it's really great.

About this time I began to have a recurring dream—or nightmare really—that I had rejected the call to serve a mission in Central America. However awful that thought was, the greatest nightmare was that this experience would never even have entered into my mind, and I never would have known what I missed. In my dream I would see the faces of the members of the branch in Totonicapan and the wonderful missionaries I had met thus far. It was so unthinkable to me that I might never have known these people and the great work that was being done among them that I would wake up night after night in a cold sweat. It went on for some time, but thankfully I eventually got over it.

In the middle of January I experienced my first baptism in Guatemala. Three people were baptized. I did the baptizing, and Elder Wilson confirmed them members of the Church. I had never baptized anyone before, and this was a sweet experience for me. It took us all day to get the *pila* (we used it for a baptismal font) ready. It was outside in our patio, and the weather was so cold that we had to heat the water. We had a big barrel, and we would fill it with water and then put it on the fire to heat. It was a lot of work but more than worth the effort. These three baptisms motivated me greatly to want to see many others come unto Christ through the waters of baptism.

We were informed that Milton R. Hunter of the Seventy was coming to Quezaltenango on January 28, 1959. Quezaltenango is about ten miles from Totonicapan, and a district-wide conference was to be held there. I looked forward to making the big trip as I had not left Totonicapan since arriving there the first part of November 1958.

It was a great experience to meet with the other elders in my district. I had really not met any of them since arriving in Totonicapan. The thing I loved the most was singing with my fellow missionaries and the testimony meeting that was followed by instruction from our mission president. Elder Hunter was very sick and unable to speak to the missionaries or interview us. We were all disappointed, but the district conference still turned out to be one of the most spiritual experiences I had had up to that point in my life. I was immersed in the Spirit, and it was difficult to get on a bus that evening and return to Totonicapan.

After that great spiritual experience, it seemed as though the adversary worked overtime to make me discouraged and to stop me from getting out of bed to study and work. I believe that a true principle is involved in this. The Savior was in the Judean wilderness fasting and praying for forty days and communing with God. When that experience ended, the adversary immediately came to tempt Christ and destroy Him. I think we can always expect that when we have had a great spiritual experience, there will be a backlash from Satan. A further illustration of this principle is found in the experience Moses had as recorded in the book of Moses in the Pearl of Great Price. He was privileged to be in the presence of God and to see in vision the heavens and all the creations made by the Almighty's hand. He was transfigured so that he could abide the presence of God. Few men have been privileged to have such an experience. Immediately after the vision closed, who should appear to Moses but the adversary, saying, "Moses, son of man, worship me" (Moses 1:12). The adversary will do everything in his power to destroy the work of God. We must continue to be on guard, especially when we have experienced great spiritual manifestations, not to be overcome by the subtle or straightforward and powerful manifestations of evil.

During these first few months of my mission in Totonicapan, I observed for the first time in the mission field what I call the "Celso Arriola Syndrome." Celso Arriola was a bodybuilder, so he was strong and well muscled. He was a Ladino, a mixture of Indian and Spanish blood. He was very active in the branch, but he had a prideful nature. He believed that his wife was having an affair with another man in the branch. His wife begged him to believe that this was not true. We counseled with him and with his wife, but it seemed that nothing my companion could say could appease Celso. It looked like the marriage was going to come apart when an interesting thing happened. Somebody in the branch started a rumor that Celso's wife was being unfaithful to him. When Celso heard this, he was incensed and felt it his duty to defend his wife's honor. This caused strife among the members of the branch for a time, but Celso's marriage was strengthened and the problem was soon forgotten. For the next two and a half years, I would see many silly problems that would divide branches and cause people to become inactive. When testimonies are not deep and strong, the least provocation can cause people to leave the Church and hold grudges that sometimes never seem to go away.

Throughout my missionary experience, I observed firsthand the parable of the sower in Matthew 13, which could better be called the parable of the four kinds of soil. The four kinds of soil, of course, represented four distinct groups of people and how they reacted to the gospel when it came to them from the Lord or through His missionaries. The Savior's parable in Matthew 13 is similar to Lehi's dream in 1 Nephi 8, in which Lehi saw four distinct groups of people and their reaction to the tree, which represented the love of God and the fruit of eternal life. In the parable of the four kinds of soil, in Lehi's dream, and on my mission I saw and experienced the four kinds of people on a daily basis. There were those who would not even pretend to listen to the word of God we were attempting to deliver to them. There were those who willingly accepted our message, but when any hint of trouble or persecution arose, they quickly fell away. Then there were those who embraced the gospel with all their hearts and were productive in building the kingdom, but then let the cares and distractions of the world choke out their faith and testimonies. And there were those who were the good, productive soil—those who went to the tree, partook of the fruit, and never were distracted by those in the great and spacious building.

Thankfully, Celso remained active in the Church, and when I finally left Totonicapan, he gave me the strongest *abrazo* (hug) I had ever received. It just about broke my back. My son John, who also served his mission in Guatemala from 1993 through 1994, returned to Guatemala in the spring of 2003 for a visit and went to Totonicapan because of my request that he do so. He arrived there on a Sunday just as one of the wards was finishing the meeting block. In talking to some of the people in the ward, he asked them who the oldest members were. One of the names they mentioned was Celso Arriola, who had just passed away a few months before John's visit. The members informed John that Celso had been active and a strong member of the Church through all the years. He was "good earth" who just needed to have a few weeds pulled out of his life, as most of us do. (There is now a stake in Totonicapan.)

In a letter from Totonicapan dated February 2, 1959, four months into my mission, I wrote the following to my parents:

> I can say now that taking piano lessons and horn lessons was the best thing I ever did, not for the music but what it taught me. It was a form of discipline, something I had to do every day, and I thank Ma for making me do it. Some of the missionaries can't get up in the morning; they can't or won't study. It's a bigger problem than you would imagine, but it's not hard for me. I get up at 5 AM every morning and study, and I like to do it.

Perhaps nothing prepared me to be a missionary more then the self-discipline that came into my life from practicing the piano and the clarinet. I knew because of practicing these instruments through the years that I could do anything for two hours and then take a break and start all over again for another two hours. As I look back from the perspective of time, I do believe that my words were accurate. That same discipline has blessed me to deal with my paralysis as I am able to read and study and write for hours at a time on my computer. What a blessing!

I also wrote in that same letter, and my sources are questionable as is sometimes the case with an overly enthusiastic missionary, but what I said then was very prophetic:

> It has been prophesied by apostles in the Church that someday great prophets would raise up out of this people, prophets and leaders greater than the apostles in the church today. It won't happen now, but in 10 or 20 years it will come to pass [obviously my prediction and not that of the apostles]. The kids in the Primary here, when they grow up and have children, those children they have will be the great people.

There is now a Guatemalan member of the Second Quorum of the Seventy, Carlos Amado, who is a great leader among his people. Over forty years have passed since I wrote that letter, and what I said then has not totally been fulfilled, but there is still the future.

One day in February 1959 we got as many members of the branch together as we could, and beginning at 7 AM we worked until 9 PM cleaning the chapel. It had a tile floor that we scrubbed on our hands and knees and then waxed by hand as well. I was exhausted but felt good in my heart for the work accomplished and the opportunity to work physically. The next day we rented horses and rode out into the countryside to the little village of Pa Qui. We had some investigators there and had started going out at least once a week. We rode these horses to save time, and of course to have a little fun. Thankfully, as a young boy my dad took me deer hunting on horseback several times, and though I was not much of an equestrian, I could ride and knew just a little bit about horses. These Guatemalan horses were not nearly as large as those I had ridden as a boy, but that was just fine with me. The smaller and slower they were, the better they were as far as I was concerned. I was in the saddle most of that day and into the night and miraculously did not get very sore. I don't know if riding horses was against mission rules—we never asked—but it added a unique dimension to my time in Totonicapan.

While in Totonicapan I developed some strong feelings about the culture that existed among the Indians and how the difficulty just to maintain life was a daily struggle for these people. It seemed to me that the little Indian women worked much harder than their husbands. I quote from a letter:

> Boy, these poor old Indian ladies down here work twice as hard as their good-for-nothing husbands. You see a bunch of Indians walking down the street, and all the men will be in front about 10 feet ahead of the women. They'll be talking and having a great time, and they won't be carrying anything. Then here comes the poor woman, with a baby strapped on her back and a big basket on her head and something in her arms. The men really give the women a bad time here. But no matter how tough things get you never ever hear one of them complain.

Infant mortality was a stark reality for almost every family. One family in the branch had lost five out of seven children to early death. Little babies didn't seem to have much of a chance because of malnutrition and unsanitary living conditions. As a young twenty-year-old, it was an eye-opening experience to see firsthand that not everybody in this world was as blessed as we were in the United States. (As the years unfold I will relate some personal experiences I had with the death and burial of babies and adult members of the Church while I was in Central America.) The bad water, lack of sanitary conditions, scarcity of good nutritious food, and the inequity that existed between the rich and the poor in Central America were appalling. Forty years later it still bothers me.

Late in February of 1959 I suffered a case of paratyphoid. It kept me in bed for three days with a very high fever and an aching body. I remember lying in bed in that room with no windows, moaning and groaning out loud when my companion was out of earshot. It seemed to give me some relief. Finally the only doctor in town took a look at me and was able to prescribe some medication that helped almost immediately. For days, however, I felt like I had been beat with a rubber hose. As a result of that brief encounter with paratyphoid, I realized that as a missionary when you are sick and can't work, you are a liability and not an asset to your companion or the missionary work.

I had arrived in Totonicapan November 9, 1958. In a letter written from Totonicapan on March 8, 1959, I wrote:

> I've been here in Totonicapan and in the mission 4 months as of the eighth of March. I have learned a great deal in that period of time. I'm getting so I can read the D&C and Book of Mormon in Spanish almost as well as in English. The Bible is a lot harder. I've learned a lot about the gospel but the thing I've learned the most is about people. I have met some great men since I have been here. The man that stands out in my mind is the president of the mission, President Edgar J. Wagner.

> He finishes his mission this month, and then we will have a new president. He is really a man inspired of God. He carries a wonderful spirit with him, and you feel elevated when in his presence. I've come to the conclusion that my life up until I came in the mission wasn't too hot in comparison with what I want to do and be now.

During this period of time some of my thoughts and feelings about missionary work began to crystallize in my mind.

> I've been here quite a while now, and I really love the work. I've really been happy in doing the Lord's work, and the days I've worked the hardest and longest have been my happiest days. Being a missionary is not an easy job. Many people you talk to don't believe a word you say; others believe but are too weak to do anything about it. It gets a little discouraging, and then you meet the person with the honest heart, the sincere person, the person with courage, and it's just like a ray of sunshine on a cloudy day.

A hunger was truly building within me to bring many souls unto Christ. It began to seem that there were not enough hours in the day to do all that needed to be done by way of preparation and proselyting.

On March 21, 1959, I received a telegram from Guatemala City informing me of my transfer to Retalhuleu, a small city on the coast that had the reputation of being the hottest (climate-wise) city in Guatemala. It was sad to leave Totonicapan and the wonderful people who had come to mean so much to me. I knew that I probably would not see any of them again, at least in this lifetime. They were a humble, believing people, and what I learned from them would bless me and help me throughout the remainder of my mission and for the rest of my life. I was also sad to leave Elder Wilson. He had been a very loving and wonderful companion in spite of the fact that he was sick so much of the time. I learned a great deal from him about the importance of loving the people. I spoke for twenty minutes in sacrament meeting the day before I left. My Spanish was coming right along. Though sad to leave, I was excited about the new experience that awaited me in Retalhuleu.

CHAPTER 6

# Retalhuleu

It seemed to me that the trip from Totonicapan to Retalhuleu was downhill all the way. Totonicapan was the highest village where we had missionaries at that time. The weather was always cool, if not cold. As I rode to the coast, I could see the vegetation changing quickly from evergreen trees to banana trees and jungle. It wasn't really a long ride as I recall, and when I finally stepped off the bus in Retalhuleu, I was convinced that indeed it was the hottest and most humid place I had ever been in my life.

I was introduced to Elder Frank Lawton, my new companion. He was called "Machine-Gun Lawton" because of his ability to speak the Spanish language with great rapidity. Elder Lawton was a good missionary, but for some reason when I first met him he was very abrasive with me. He would ask me a question, and I would say, "Huh?" He would then say that he didn't like people who said "huh." I would then say "*Huh*?" Well, this went on for the first couple of days, and I did not know how I could endure the heat and Elder Lawton. I wrote my parents on March 25, 1959:

> I really prayed, I don't know for how long but when I quit, there came a calm feeling over me. Peace—it's hard to describe, but when I got up in the morning everything was great. Since that day, Elder Lawton and I have grown to be very close friends. I had to give a little, and he had to as well, but I think the Lord did the most.

Elder Lawton could speak great Spanish. He took it as his goal to help me improve my speaking of the Spanish language. Every talk I gave and every discussion I participated in, he would take notes of all my mistakes and go over them with me when we had time. I must admit that it was a bit disconcerting to have him constantly taking notes and criticizing my Spanish, but I swallowed my pride and tried to learn from him. He bought a Spanish *Reader's Digest*, and every morning before leaving the house he would make vocabulary cards with unusual words on them. As we walked through the streets we would test each other on these words. Forty years later, I still know the Spanish word for *machine gun*, *wicker basket*, and *shower*.

Retalhuleu was a big city compared to Totonicapan, and most of the streets were paved. The people were better educated, but the work was still not easy. Today there is a large stake in Retalhuleu, but then there was just a small branch in a rented home. We lived in a room above the chapel; it was a much nicer place than the room I had in Totonicapan. When I sat at my desk at 5 AM, there would be big pools of sweat underneath my arms as they rested on the desktop. I have never felt such heat and humidity.

I had a dark black wool suit as well as a blue wool suit. By then I had lost considerable weight and had purchased a pair of suspenders to hold up my pants. The mission rule was that we had to wear a full suit and hat regardless of our location. We would leave the house early in the morning with our suits on and return at noon to take a shower and put on our dry suit. At night I would hang my pants up by the suspenders on a nail. As the moisture evaporated, the suspenders would shrink so that in the morning they would pull the waistline of my pants up around my chest. By noon my pant legs would be dragging on the ground, and they represented just a little bit the way I felt in that horrible heat. The missionaries were easily identifiable as the two black blobs in a city in which everybody else wore white or very little of anything. You could see somebody coming down the street literally leaving a wake behind them because of the high humidity. One of the members of the branch was a tailor, and he offered to make me a new lightweight suit for thirty dollars. I took him up on it. Fortunately there was a Dairy Freeze in town, and we gave them a lot of business.

My first Sunday in the branch I played a piano solo, "The Dream of Olwen." Everybody seemed to enjoy it. Later in the week I had the opportunity of meeting John O'Donnal, whom I mentioned at the beginning of this book. At the time I didn't realize who he was and the significant contribution he had made and would yet make in establishing the Church in Guatemala. I got to know him quite well. His wife, Carmen, was the first native Guatemalan to be baptized into the Church. John had performed the baptism. He and Carmen lived in a beautiful home a few miles from Retalhuleu on a rubber plantation he managed. Through the eyes of a very young missionary, Brother O'Donnal was a very imposing figure. He impressed me in many ways. He spoke Spanish like a native, which inspired me to try to master the language as he had. We had a district missionary and testimony meeting at his plantation and were served a delicious dinner. To give you an insight into the kind of economic situation I grew up with, I was impressed beyond belief that John O'Donnal paid two hundred dollars in tithing every couple of months to my missionary companion who was serving as the branch president. I wrote in a letter to my parents, "So you can see that he's not poor."

I was very impressed with the beauty of that part of Guatemala. Soon after my arrival in town we had a special baptism. The man was Julian Reyes, and he was baptized along with his wife in a river that ran through a farm just outside of Retalhuleu. It certainly was an idyllic setting with the countryside being so green and lush. Brother Reyes was an intelligent man and had a great knowledge of the Bible and of the gospel. I saw him as a potential leader, and I wonder what he has done over the years.

The Sunday after this baptism, as we were sitting in sacrament meeting, a little old lady with a cane hobbled into the chapel. We had visited her during the week and had given her the first discussion and invited her to come to church. She had walked that morning over a mile to come to church, which must have taken her a couple of hours. My take on her was *she's really old and smart too, and she has lots of guts. I'll bet she gets baptized someday.*

Later that week we had a district conference in Mazatenango, just a few miles away from Retalhuleu. There were about 180 people in attendance, which was the biggest group of Latter-day Saints I had seen gathered together since my arrival in Guatemala. I also met our new mission president, Victor C. Hancock. He reminded me of Santa Claus. He was big, round, and jolly, and he made you feel good just to be around him. He was quite a contrast to President Wagner. President Wagner was a great mission president, but he was much more formal and reserved than President Hancock. President Wagner laid a solid foundation for what President Hancock would accomplish in terms of convert baptisms during his administration. President Hancock was a teacher of foreign languages at Weber State College. He spoke Italian, French, German, Spanish, and two or three other languages. His Spanish was very formal and educated—beautiful to listen to. I was impressed at that early stage of my mission with his language ability. It is very interesting what you remember over the years. During the first talk I heard him give at that district conference, he said something I will never forget. I can only remember the English translation. I wish I could recall it in Spanish because it is so much more beautiful in that language. It goes something like this: "The water in the ocean is salty and bitter, but as it evaporates and rises closer to heaven it becomes sweet and gives life as rain to all the earth. This is what the gospel does to us." My first district conference was a wonderful experience.

The districts in the mission were similar to stakes in that a number of branches formed a district. District presidents were usually full-time elders, but John O'Donnal was called as president of the Mazatenango District. For several Sundays in a row he would take me with him to visit some of the small branches and give piano lessons to the ward organists. I couldn't do too much with them in the little time I had, but I did try to help them as best I could. As my mission went on, in every assignment I had, I was increasingly grateful that I had learned to play the piano as a young man. It became one of the most important assets I brought into the mission field. Being able to play the piano was a bridge that immediately united me with member and nonmember alike. I discovered that music really is the universal language.

MAY 10, 1959

This is truly a wonderful work that we are doing down here, and it's hard too. We had a man all ready for baptism; Gonzalo Sanchez is his name. We had the date set for the 16th of May, just six weeks away. Last night he didn't come to sacrament meeting. It was the first time he had missed in about three months. We thought something was wrong with him, and after the meeting two of the members came and told

> us that they had seen him drunk in the street. It is really sad, because before this he was a big alcoholic. We have to go see him tonight and tell him that we can't baptize him for at least three months. I wonder what happened to him.

Several things come to mind as I read this now. The first is how stringent we were in offering baptism to people. I doubt this would happen today. We probably would have baptized him within three months, and even if he had gotten drunk one night I doubt we would have waited three additional months to baptize him. This is not my opinion regarding whether it was right or wrong to wait so long, just an observation. Second, "what happened to him" is that Satan was working very hard among those Lamanite people to keep the work from progressing. He knew what would happen to these great people if they accepted the gospel. The strength of the Church in that land today is proof of that statement.

## CHAPTER 7

# *Tecpan*

On May 12, 1959, I was sitting at my desk studying around 6 AM when two elders from Mazatenango banged on the door, came into the room, and told me that I was supposed to be in Guatemala City. They had sent me a telegram, which somehow they realized had never arrived, so they had come to help me pack my bags and catch the first possible bus to Guatemala City. I was able to get on a 9 AM bus and arrived at the city at 4 PM. I was happy and surprised to see Elder Peter Prina, one of my best friends from Ely, Nevada. We had gone to high school together. He was working in the mission office, and it was wonderful to see a familiar face from home. I was impressed with him, and he struck me as being an outstanding missionary.

The mission president called me into his office and told me he had intended to send me to Honduras, but I had missed the plane because of the mix-up with the telegram. He informed me that instead he was sending me to the Indian village of Tecpan to be the senior companion and branch president. I almost fell out of my chair and immediately felt sick to my stomach. As it is in life, so it is in the mission field. Small, seemingly insignificant events such as the non-delivery of a telegram can change an entire mission experience. I have always wondered what my mission and life would have been had I not been sent to Tecpan. Had I gone to Honduras, I never would have had the privilege of working as long as I did with the Mayan Indian people in the mountains of Guatemala. I think the Lord wanted me to have that experience, not only for what it would do for me as a missionary but also for some qualities I would develop that would bless my life forever.

President Hancock took me immediately to the bus station. My Spanish still was not very good, and the president had to tell the bus driver where to let me off in Tecpan so that I could meet my new companion. It was one of those buses in which the seats had been put closer together so that they could fit more people on the bus. The Indians were short, so it didn't bother them, but it was always a challenge for us missionaries. We tried to get the seats at the front of the bus so that we could stretch out our legs. The bus I rode to Tecpan was named *La Dama Tecpaneca,* which means "the Tecpan Lady."

It was about a three-hour trip, and it was dark when I arrived. Tecpan was a little Indian village, much smaller than Totonicapan. Because it was late at night, I couldn't get a good feeling for what it looked like. The bus driver stopped the bus in the middle of the street and pointed at a house, which I assumed was where my companion would be waiting for me. As the bus stopped, my companion came to the door of the house and walked over to help me with my luggage. He was Elder Reed Bentley from St. George, Utah. He had been told that his new companion had been in the mission for almost two and a half years and did not know about the mix-up with transfers. Elder Bentley had only been in the mission field for five months—about one month fewer than I. He went pale when he realized that his new senior companion was as green as he was and couldn't speak Spanish any better. We got inside our room, shut the door, and just stared at each other. We were both scared to death. Later that night I observed Elder Bentley writing a letter to his parents. He left the room for a minute, and I glanced at the letter in which he had written that his new companion had just arrived and that he didn't know anything about missionary work and couldn't speak the language any better than he could. He went on to write that he just didn't know what we were going to do. I have to admit that he was right on target. I came to love Elder Bentley as much as any companion I ever had because of his honest and forthright manner.

We had good living accommodations in Tecpan. Although it was a little village, a rich man from Guatemala City, who was out of favor with the government, had come to Tecpan many years before and built a hotel. He also had built, adjacent to the hotel, a little house made of brick that served as the chapel and included the room in which we lived. It was one of the few rooms I ever had during my mission that had its own shower and hot water. The drawback, however, was that our mattresses were infested with fleas. To protect ourselves we would tuck our pajamas into our socks so that there was no flesh available to the fleas. We would also sprinkle flea powder all over our sheets each night before getting into bed. If we did not do these things, the fleas would almost carry us away during the night. We also ate at the hotel, but the food was less than desirable. The owner's name was Don Guillermo, and he was a character. He was probably in his seventies and had white hair. He enjoyed speaking to us but was a million miles away from ever becoming a member of the Church. He was probably the best-educated man in that little Indian village.

*Don Guillermo, hotel owner in Tecpan.*

I was very humbled by my new calling, and the thing that helped me the most was a phrase from my patriarchal blessing that if I was living the commandments I would never be given a job in the Church or any assignment that I would be unable to do.

There were only twelve members in the branch when I arrived. One of the problems I recognized right away was that the Indians in Tecpan spoke very poor Spanish. In our sacrament meetings we would speak in Spanish and then have it translated into Cachiquel, the Indian dialect in that part of Guatemala. Typically the men spoke poor Spanish, and the women didn't speak it at all. In my first sacrament meeting in Tecpan, I gave a talk and played a piano solo. As I still couldn't speak Spanish very well, I think that the piano solo lasted longer than my talk. During that first Sunday I taught the priesthood class and also the Sunday School class, and on Tuesday evening I taught a class on the Book of Mormon. This was very difficult for me to do. I would write out my talks and lessons in English and then translate them before I would deliver them in public.

MAY 25, 1959

> This is really a struggle right now because of the language, but I am talking quite well for the time that I have had in the mission, and I know that with the help of the Lord and if I am humble I will be able to do everything that I have to.

That same day, I wrote how good it was to be the senior companion. It seemed like a lot of responsibility, but at the same time it was good to be on my own and to do my own thinking and planning.

The Indians in Tecpan had a gambling and drinking problem. They would gather in groups on the street, and then they would roll a bone. One side was smooth and the other side rough, and they bet on which side would come up. I must admit that I was a little disillusioned with the Indians of Tecpan. It seemed to me that they spent a third of their time drinking, a third of their time sobering up, and a third of their time rolling bones (gambling). Tecpan was a far cry from Totonicapan. It boasted one large general store, the typical Catholic cathedral, some municipal buildings, and a few small business establishments, all of which surrounded—or I should say made up—the square in the middle of the village.

I soon realized that this was the toughest job I had ever experienced. The first missionaries in Tecpan really intimidated these humble Indian people. They were too aggressive in their proselyting techniques. It turned these people off, and the local Catholic priest added to the problem by frightening them with stories of the Mormon missionaries capturing their women and carrying them off to the United States. There were two other Indian villages in those mountains just a few miles apart that were prospering in terms of convert baptisms. I believe it all had to do with the missionaries who opened those villages to missionary work.

All the streets in this village were dirty and dusty during the non-rainy season and filled with mud during the rainy season. It seemed that every family had numerous dogs and that they all had been trained to hate the missionaries. They were a constant threat as we walked the streets of that little village. We learned the technique of staring these dogs down. As you established eye contact with them and walked toward them, they would put their tails between their legs and run off howling. The thing that kept me working hard in spite of these and other challenges was how sweet the twelve members of the branch were. It was so obvious to me the incredible change the gospel brought into the lives of these people as they repented, were baptized, and received the Holy Ghost into their lives.

I was saddened by their poverty. The men would work from dawn to dusk in the fields for fifty cents a day. Their diet consisted mainly of corn tortillas. Even the dogs were fed corn tortillas. Infant mortality was a constant specter hovering over the people. They lived in adobe huts that had grass roofs with no chimneys to expel the smoke coming from the little fire built in the middle of the dirt floor. At least once each day they would walk to the center plaza, or square, where there was a large *pila* (fountain) to

fill their large jugs with water. The is was the work of the women, and they carried the jugs on their heads as they did almost everything else that had to be transported.

Tecpan was a primitive village. All the work was done by hand, and whatever needed to be transported was transported on people's heads or backs, or by old ox carts and ox teams. It was like going back in time to the eighteenth or nineteenth century. The people told us that they even dressed much as the Indians had dressed for hundreds of years in those mountains. The women from each village could be identified by the color of the blouse they wore. They weaved their own cloth, and the way the women of each village dressed was very distinct. The patterns for the cloth had been passed down through the years from mothers to daughters.

There is no way around it. The missionary work in Tecpan was difficult. We would leave the house by 5 AM so that we could visit with the men before they went to the fields to work. We would sit around the little fire they had in the middle of the floor and try to teach them the discussions while they were getting something to eat before going out in the fields to swing a hoe for ten or twelve hours. As you can imagine, these discussions were not very productive. We were working sixty hours or more every week and only getting twenty-five visits.

I wrote, "Actually it's kind of fun. I would rather talk to these old Indian women than any other people in the world. They are really funny. They really have a sense of humor."

I arrived in Tecpan right in the middle of the rainy season. The rain never seemed to stop. The streets were like rivers and were difficult to cross. When water was not running through the streets, the streets were filled with mud. I later learned when the rainy season ended and the dry season began, the same streets would be nothing but dust. It was always difficult to be clean in Tecpan. We always smelled like we had been camping because of the campfires in the people's huts. The sad thing about Tecpan was the people truly were afraid of us. We would go to the post office or the general store, and the minute we walked in, it would become deathly silent. I began to genuinely dislike the Catholic Church at this time, not the people but the organization. I know that the Catholic Church has done much good during its history in many parts of the world, but what I observed in Central America left me with few positive feelings regarding Catholicism. The priests had kept these beautiful Indian people in ignorance for so many years that when the truth was brought to them they were in no position to open their minds or their hearts to receive it. None of the women knew how to read, and most of the men were illiterate as well. Few of them had a Bible in their home, and what they knew about the gospel came from the priests. The priests, of course, did everything in their power to convince the people to not let us into their homes or listen to our message. To do penance, an individual who had come for confession would sometimes sit out on the steps in front of the church and beat on a drum for hours at a time. Another act of penance was to stand in front of the church and play a flute made out of a willow or some kind of reed. To this day when I reflect back in my mind about the time I spent in Tecpan, I can hear the beating of the drum and the sound of the flute, which represented to me the ignorance and poverty with which the Catholic Church, over the centuries, had kept these sweet people in abject slavery.

JUNE 21, 1959

Happy Father's Day, Dad. I know Father's Day is in June sometime and is probably already passed, but happy Father's Day anyway. Thanks, Dad, for all that you have done for me; I really appreciate it. Many times we don't take time to tell people what we think of them when we really should. I would just like to take this chance to tell you that I think you are a pretty good old guy and that when the time comes I hope I can be half as good a dad to my kids as you've been to me.

I have gotten over the diarrhea for a while, but my companion has got it worse than I did. Last Friday we had to go to Guatemala City to see a doctor. Guatemala City is about a three-hour ride from Tecpan by bus. Part of the way is on a dirt road. Boy, you ought to see Guatemala City. It's a lot bigger than Salt Lake City and very modern also. It seemed like being back in the states. You just can't imagine that in the

> same country there can be such big differences between towns. Tecpan is like living in the old horse and buggy days. Only a few houses have toilets or electrical lights, and it's dirty, and then Guatemala City is just beautiful. My companion and I were just like a couple of old sheepherders headed for town for the first time. The first thing we did was go to a Dairy Freeze and eat ice cream. Then we went to a place called Pecos Bills and ate hamburgers and footlong hot dogs and milkshakes. I thought I was going to get sicker than a dog, but I didn't. That food, after eating the food in Tecpan, tasted better than any Thanksgiving dinner I have ever eaten, and that is saying a lot.

Reading this letter from June 1959, it's interesting how my perspective regarding Guatemala City had changed since I first stepped off the airplane in November of 1958. Sociologists call this phenomenon "relative deprivation." The Indians, many of whom had never visited Guatemala City, didn't miss anything that the city had to offer. However, those of us who came from a society like the United States, which had everything, felt deprived living among the Indians. I'm sure Guatemala City was still just as dirty and run down in many areas as it was when President Wagner drove me in the mission Buick through the streets from the airport to the mission home. Only now, after months in the mission field, it looked a lot like Camelot.

The doctor discovered that Elder Bentley had amoebas and parasites inside him, and with the medicine he was given he began to feel much better. I fought dysentery my entire mission. You were never really totally free of it, and it was just one of the facts of life that you dealt with as you did missionary work in the mountains of Guatemala. The mission joke was, "I only got sick once on my mission to Central America. I got sick the first day I arrived and was sick until I left."

In Tecpan we were part of the Chimaltenango District, which also included the Indian villages of Patzicia and Patzun. These were very small villages except for Chimaltenango, which was much larger and could have had five to seven thousand people living in it. Looking back at it now, it is difficult for me to judge the population of any of these villages, but they were small. One day we received a telegram from the elders who were working in Patzicia, which was a short distance from Tecpan. The elders had to leave town to take care of some business. They asked my companion and me to catch the bus and come down and preside over a wedding reception in the branch. Two Indians had gotten married after living together for fifteen years and having a family of four children. This was not uncommon, and their marriage was the cause of great rejoicing to all the members in the branch because the next day the family would all be baptized. Though Tecpan and Patzicia were close together geographically, they were miles apart spiritually. Patzicia had a thriving branch of over sixty members, and it was so fun to share that evening with them. Elder Bentley and I both spoke, and our talks were translated into the Indian dialect. Afterward we had a little party and were treated like kings. They loved the elders and felt that they were true messengers of God. It was a very humbling experience to sit at the head of the table and eat food that was so precious to them, and yet they wanted to give all they had to the missionaries. I fell in love with these pure Lamanite people. I was fortunate to spend so much time with them. Many missionaries in Central America never had the opportunity of working in the mountains with the Indians. What a blessing it was to me to have this great opportunity! To this day I love them, and they will always have a special place in my heart. When I came home from my mission, it took a long time to adjust to the ways of Anglo-Saxons. I still have a great affinity for Hispanics and Indians. I related well to them and still do today. Had I not had my accident, I wonder if Jo Anne and I

*Baptismal service in Patzicia.*

would have had the opportunity of serving a mission among these special people. That question, of course, will never be answered.

We broke with the tradition of the former elders in Tecpan and changed our eating arrangements. They had been eating at the same location for several years, but we found a place that looked a little better.

> We have beans three times a day. It's the custom of the people. They do have a lot of eggs every morning, also cornflakes and hot milk and bananas. The other two meals, no telling what we have, just about everything. We have many native dishes such as tacos, chuchus, tamales, rice, and beans—hard, mashed, fried, and baked.

I was impressed that we could hire a woman to wash all our clothes and iron them every week for three dollars apiece per month. I was able to get a haircut for twenty-five cents. They used the old hand clippers, but I thought they did a pretty good job under the circumstances. Labor was so cheap that even on the limited amount of money we were allowed to spend as missionaries, we lived like kings in comparison to most of the inhabitants of Tecpan.

There was a young eleven-year-old boy by the name of Mario who worked in the restaurant where we ate each day. He worked eleven hours a day and then would go to school at night. He still was unable to read, and I felt great sorrow for the kind of life that he was forced to live. Frankly, I saw little hope that these people could ever improve their lot in life. Membership in the Church at least filled them with hope in Heavenly Father's plan of happiness even though it was literally impossible for most of them to improve their lot economically. Mario had to work such long hours so his family could buy enough corn tortillas to eat each day. I was embarrassed at my relative affluence.

JULY 13, 1959

> Today I completed two months in Tecpan, and on the sixth I completed eight months in the mission. It has really gone by fast, as the time always does when you're working hard.

The week before, we had a missionary meeting in Patzicia. Today it would have been called a district meeting. There were eight elders and the mission presidency in attendance. It was always a special treat to be with President Hancock because of his positive and pleasant personality. To me some of the best meetings I have ever attended in which I felt the Spirit strongly were missionary meetings in the mission field. I especially loved to sing the hymns with the elders.

I have to comment about Sister Hancock at this time. She was the sweetest woman you could ever meet. However, she had an aversion to dirt, and you could see that it took lots of self-discipline for her to shake the hands of these Indian people in Patzicia. The mission home was immaculate. She was a good cook and mothered the missionaries with all of her heart, but she never did feel at home with the Latin American culture. She made no attempt to learn Spanish, but I do think that her contribution to the health and welfare of the missionaries was enormous. Whenever we ate at the mission home, she set a high standard with regard to our table manners. Many was the missionary that got a slap on the hand for being sloppy at the table or reaching too far for the jam and one of her incredible homemade rolls. I am sure she breathed a great sigh of relief when she was able to leave Central America and rejoin her family in Ogden, Utah. I don't wish to misrepresent her in any way, and just let me say that she was a loving, devoted, faithful, Latter-day Saint woman—the kind who has helped to hold the Church and families together from the beginning of this dispensation.

We kept working and were invited into a few more homes, but the people were not at all receptive to our message. It was discouraging, but we just kept trying as hard as we could. If the measure of a missionary's success is the number of convert baptisms he brings into the Church, then my time in Tecpan was a total failure. On the other hand, if success is measured by personal growth and increased self-discipline, then Tecpan was undoubtedly my most successful assignment. As I look back on it now, my time in Tecpan was an important time of preparation, not only for future assignments in the mission field but for life itself. In the relative quiet and obscurity of this isolated Indian village, my knowledge of Spanish grew, my work ethic increased, my relationship with the Lord deepened, and when I finally left Tecpan, which wouldn't take place for another four months, I was prepared for an assignment of greater responsibility.

Although not pleasant at the time, what a great learning experience it was for me to be in the minority and hated and feared by the majority. Any racist attitudes I had developed while growing up faded away because of my Tecpan experience. Since being paralyzed and confined to a wheelchair, I feel how it is to be different from the majority. It doesn't bother me that much, but I am empathetic to the plight of the disabled.

We simply cannot do enough for them. I can see a preparation that took place during my mission for what I would be called on to experience later in life. I am grateful for the growth that comes from difficult experiences. To show how young and impetuous I was, while in Tecpan I would pray, saying, "If there is any assignment more difficult than this in this mission, I will volunteer for it. With Thy help, I know I can do it." Come to think of it, maybe that's an attitude we all should have regardless of whether we are young and impetuous.

> July 19, 1959
>
> The Lord really blessed us last week. We worked 64 hours and got 25 cottage meetings. They say that things are always darkest before the sunshine breaks through, and last week we really got some wonderful meetings. We have about four pretty honest people that might be baptized someday, Señor Rios and Señora Santos especially, and then young kids of 16 years old. Also, we are teaching an old guy that belongs to the Baptist Church. He's been baptized three different times in different churches, but now I think he can see that they didn't count. The only trouble is that he's so old.

Working that many hours in such a small town (I estimated the population at 1,500 but it could have been larger), we would finally get to the point that we knew what to expect at almost each door. The street that led to the cemetery was the most difficult in Tecpan. The street began at the Catholic cathedral, and any time there was a funeral, which was frequently, the procession would go down that street to the cemetery. Almost every home on that street produced and sold items that were used by the Catholic Church in the burial process and the funeral ceremony. Also, a number of the homes produced the fireworks that were an integral part of every Catholic celebration. You could count on being rejected with hostility at any of those homes on that street. Whenever the district president or the assistants to the president would come to work with us, we would always take them to that street, not telling them beforehand what we knew would happen and then feigning surprise at the reception we encountered at each door.

Sometimes we would get so discouraged with the few quality visits we would get from day to day that we would go out into the fields and give our discussions to the cattle. I have given many third and fourth discussions to cows so that I would not forget the discussions. As difficult as it was, however, it was in Tecpan I came to understand why Guatemala

is called the land of eternal spring. It truly was a delightful climate. It was never too cold or hot. We always began our day before the sun came up, and when it finally did come up behind those beautiful mountains, the early morning hours were so pure and clean. What can compare to walking down a dirt road with fields of corn on every side surrounded by mountains and forest? The roosters would be crowing, and smoke would begin to emanate from the adobe homes that dotted the countryside. It was a hard life, but at least it was lived in an almost magical setting as far as I was concerned. I wrote in this July 19 letter that the altitude was 7,800 feet. I'm not sure where I got my information or how accurate that figure is, but we were in the mountains.

> JULY 19, 1959
>
> These Indians take off early, and so we have to go to work early. We never get any visits after 7:30 PM because they are all in bed. I'm working hard, the time is going by fast, and I know that if I'm faithful and clean the Lord will help me. We can't do anything without the Lord's help because it's His work and not a work of man.

About five miles outside of Tecpan were the ruins of the ancient city of Iximche. Many hundreds of years before, Iximche had been the capital city of all the Mayan Indians in that part of Guatemala. A group of archaeologists from a number of different countries were working on the ruins. Having an investigator nearby was our excuse for walking out to Iximche almost every week. We would visit the investigator and of course to see the ruins. It really was a fascinating place, and the archaeologists would point out to us the fortifications and how the city was put together in ancient times. The archaeologists believed that Iximche had been a great center of population in that part of Guatemala. It had been an extremely large city that was vital to all of the people living

in the surrounding area. As missionaries, we believed it to be the Book of Mormon city of Zarahemla. Every Thursday the little village of Tecpan doubled and tripled in size as the Indians came out of the hills carrying on their backs and heads produce they had grown on their little farms and items they had manufactured in their homes. This tradition had been going on as far back as the oldest natives in Tecpan could remember. Thursday for some reason was the great market day in Tecpan. The archaeologists believed it was because the tradition had begun hundreds of years ago during the times when Iximche played such a prominent role in the lives of the people living in that mountainous area. One of my visits to Iximche was reported in an August 2, 1959, letter:

> The other day the president of the district (Elder Johns) came up to work with me, and Elder Bentley went down to Patzicia for a week. We've had lots of fun during the week. Thursday we walked out to Iximche to visit an investigator we had out there. Well, when we got there we couldn't find the investigator, it seems as though he has moved. . . . We were looking around the ruins, and all of a sudden it started to rain, one of these old gully washers. Well, Elder Johns and I had to find cover fast, and the only thing that was available was an old unoccupied chicken coop. We crawled into it and talked for a while, and then I noticed some little white things crawling all over me. They were lice. Well, we hurried on out of there, but for two days we were fighting lice and just finally got the best of them.

AUGUST 2, 1959

I weighed myself Saturday on the scales of Don Guillermo, the owner of the place where we live and eat. I weighed in at 156 pounds, all ringside too. I told old Don Guillermo that he'd better start fattening me up, so I wrote my weight down, and he was going to bet me that next month I would weigh five pounds more. I told him that for every pound I gained I would give him five dollars, but if I lost or stayed the same I wouldn't have to pay him for my board. He wouldn't bet me.

During the month of August 1959, we had a district conference for all the members and investigators in Chimaltenango. Chimaltenango is about fifty miles from Tecpan, so we rented a bus, *La Estrellita de Plata* (the Little Silver Star). It was really a good bus. As I have indicated before, most of the buses here in Guatemala have names that are written on the bumpers and on the sides.

> The bus owners really take care of them, and every minute they aren't running, they are polishing them. They treat the buses better than the kids. We took 40 people from Tecpan, and that's pretty good from a branch of only 13 members. The rest were all investigators. There were about 300 people at the conference, and about 90 percent were pure Lamanites. Many talks were given by the people in the Indian dialect, Cachiquel. The people in this part of Guatemala all speak Cachiquel.

> AUGUST 9, 1959
>
> These are chosen people, and they come from the tribe of Joseph—the same Joseph that was sold into Egypt—and because of the faithfulness of Joseph it was promised him that his descendants would be a great and mighty people and would never be destroyed. They never have been either, and one day they will raise themselves up and be a great people. Right now they are still living under the curse that the Lord put on Laman, but they are gradually throwing off this curse.
>
> I've really been blessed to have been able to have come here to Guatemala, among the Indian people. I'll have to admit that I've been very discouraged at times because of the littleness of the town and the hardness of the town. I have been blessed a lot in my life, and I think the Lord has blessed me with persistence. I don't know how long I'll be here with this people, but I'm going to give it all I've got for as long as I can.

One day in August of 1959, Elder Bentley and I made a chocolate cake. Actually Elder Bentley made the cake while I watched him. We couldn't find any powdered sugar for the icing, but all the same it tasted as good as any chocolate cake I have ever eaten. His mother sent him the recipe. We took it up into the mountains and sat beneath a tree and ate the entire cake in one sitting. When we came down from the mountain, a telegram was waiting for Elder Bentley telling him of his new assignment and transfer from Tecpan. This turned out to be the hardest part of my mission—having a companion taken from me and transferred to a new assignment. I had really grown to love Elder Bentley. He was from St. George, Utah, and his father was one of the financial officers at Dixie College. Elder Bentley was a very down-to-earth guy, and I got along with him as well as any companion I had during my mission.

*Serech family. Marguerita, front left.*

> I guess the reason we got to know each other so well is because it's tough here, and we've had to really help each other. It seems like every time he gets to feeling a little sorry for himself, I feel great and help him along, and vice versa.

In our little branch in Tecpan we had only thirteen members. Seven of them were from one family, the only family that had been converted in the three years the missionaries had been in this little town. The family name was Serech. This family was persecuted from the very day they were baptized into the Church. Their neighbors quit talking to them, and everybody in town just ignored them. When they first got baptized, the elders had to stand guard over them as they washed their clothes in the river so they wouldn't get mobbed. One day two drunken neighborhood ladies broke into the house when Sister Serech was home alone. They had a bottle of whiskey and were going to make her drink it.

> AUGUST 19, 1959
>
> Sister Serech is really a tough old gal, and she didn't like these two women in the first place, so when they tried to force her to drink the booze, she turned those two old gals every way but loose. She really worked them over. Well, the police came and threw Sister Serech and the family in jail for fighting even though it wasn't her fault. They were in jail about two months before they finally got out. Everybody is against them because they are Mormons.
>
> They have a daughter, Margarita Serech, who is 17 years old. She was working in the local drugstore, and the other day she had to go to Guatemala City with the owner's wife to help buy some things they needed in the store. The owner's wife is a strong member of the Central

> American Church, which is about the worst church I have ever laid eyes on. She didn't like Margarita at all, and when they got to Guatemala City that night she made Margarita go to the Central American Church with her. Well, they were sitting there in the meeting when the preacher said that there was a Mormon in the house. He said they wanted to help her because she was in the church of the devil and they wanted to give her salvation. They said they were sorry for her and if she would renounce the Mormon Church and raise her hand and accept the Central American Church, she would be on her way to salvation. Then they really started giving her a bad time. They told her that Joseph Smith was a false prophet and a prophet of the devil and things like that. Finally she got up and walked up to the front of the building. There were about 300 people there, and before all those people she bore them her testimony that Joseph was a prophet of God, that God had a body like we do, and that Jesus was the Christ. She told them she had been baptized in the Church of Christ and that she was going to die in that church and that if anybody belonged to the church of the devil it was them.

Margarita was an incredible young lady. She had courage and she had little support in terms of a church organization. Needless to say, the members of the Central American Church did not like what she said, and the owner's wife made her sleep outside in the cold. She got sick during the night so she quit the job and came home. She couldn't get another job because the people in Tecpan wouldn't hire Mormons. I wrote home, "But there is a girl with a testimony, just a good old Lamanite that's thrown off the curse."

On August 21, 1959, I had the privilege of going to Guatemala City to a missionary meeting. The meeting took place early Saturday morning, so we had to leave Tecpan on Friday. We arrived in Guatemala City Friday evening and were privileged to stay at a legitimate hotel. We had some spare time in the evening, so we went to see a double feature at a local movie theater. This was not against the mission rules, and it was the first movie I had seen for nine months. It was a good diversion. For about the first two years of my mission, we had no official preparation day, so any kind of break in our normal routine was a blessing. The missionary meeting we had the next morning was a great experience for me as were all of the meetings with the elders and sister missionaries. There were about thirty elders and six sister missionaries in attendance. The meeting began at 8:30 AM and didn't end until 1:30 PM. President Hancock spoke to us, and we all had the opportunity of bearing our testimonies. I was always impressed with President Hancock and the good counsel he gave to us as well as the great spirit of love he always exhibited.

I liked my new companion a great deal. Elder Bentley was short and stocky, while Elder Jack Reeves, my new companion, was six feet three inches tall. I felt that I looked like a midget walking by his side down the streets of Tecpan. Compared to the Indian people, he was a giant. Elder Reeves was extremely intelligent and loved to study. I shared that same love, so we got a lot of studying done.

AUGUST 23, 1959

In about a month I'll be 21 years old and I can truthfully say it has really been an eventful year. I have learned a great deal about people and have grown to love them. I have learned how to speak Spanish and many other things I didn't think I could do.

AUGUST 30, 1959

I had kind of a tough week last week it seems. I got mad for about the first time in my mission. We got a visit with some guy quite a while ago. He didn't impress us too much, but the town is so little that you have to visit everybody. Well, last week we knocked and he came to the door. He really is a wise guy. He was laughing at us, but he invited us in just to make fun. To him we are just a big joke. I gave him the Joseph Smith story, and he really got a kick out of that—didn't believe a word of it. That really got me mad, and I started to tell him how the cow ate the cabbage. I told him that we have a word for guys like him in English called "wise guy." He didn't know what that meant, so I proceeded to explain to him in Spanish what a wise guy is. He didn't like it, and before many minutes my companion and I were outside. No matter how much satisfaction you gain from chewing someone out, it doesn't help you to further the Lord's work. No matter how obnoxious someone gets, you just have to take it. I would like to write you what David O. McKay said about prayer one time: "Many of us lose confidence in prayer because we do not realize the answer. We ask for strength, and God gives difficulties, which make us strong. We pray for wisdom, and God gives problems, a solution of which develops wisdom. We plead for prosperity, and God gives us brain and brawn with which to work. We plead for courage, and God gives us dangers to overcome. We ask for favors, and God gives us opportunities." I know that in this incident I had received an answer to prayer. I had been praying for patience, and the Lord was giving me many opportunities to develop it in Tecpan.

I received a letter from my mom about this time in which she counseled me to be humble and prayerful in doing my missionary work. I had learned by that time that what she said was absolutely true. We simply cannot do missionary work without the Lord's help, and I came to learn that this is true in all endeavors in life as well. His help comes as we humble ourselves and seek him in prayer. Receiving the call to be a senior companion and branch president simultaneously so early in my mission may have gone to my head a little, and I felt that my mom's advice was right on target. She probably picked up something from my letters that prompted this counsel.

SEPTEMBER 6, 1959

The other day Elder Reeves and I left the house at 5:30 AM as usual to go out tracting. On the first door we knocked, a man came to the door and just really called us everything he could think of (everything bad, that is). He was really mad and told us never to come back. The next door we knocked on, the very same thing happened. The man told us to hit the road and never come back. It makes you feel kind of sad sometimes to see the way some of these people have completely shut their minds and their hearts to the gospel. At times the work in Tecpan gets me down just a little, but I know if I keep trying the Lord will help me to get into these Lamanite people's doors.

As I think of this entry I am not surprised that anybody would be upset with us knocking on their door at 5:30 AM. To have a prearranged appointment would be one thing, but I can only imagine that I would be a little testy if two missionaries banged on my door at 5:30 AM. At the time, however, it was pure rejection.

SEPTEMBER 13, 1959

I have been here in Tecpan for four months now, and I believe that I have learned more during these four months than at any other time in my life. I have learned many of them the hard way and am still learning each day many new things about people and myself that will help me all my life. I think I can see now what kind of school the school of hard knocks is. It is a pretty good school too.

I'll tell you that it's tough work up here in Tecpan. I made a vow that I would never complain about where I worked, and I'm not doing it now, but this is the toughest job I've ever had. I know that I was called to work in this town for a wise purpose, and I know that if I keep trying hard, when I get in another town the work will seem about ten times easier.

*Brother Campos, only male member in Tecpan Branch, and Elder Rushton.*

This would prove to be a prophetic statement. After Tecpan every other assignment for the rest of my mission seemed easy by comparison. I can only imagine how difficult it might have been to begin my mission, for example, in Guatemala City where the living was good and the baptisms were numerous and then be transferred to a place like Tecpan. I think it would be difficult for a missionary to survive that. President Hancock was inspired.

On Sunday, September 13, 1959, we had a branch conference in Tecpan. It was the first branch conference since I had gone to Tecpan. President Hancock and his wife, along with Elder Sidney M. Johns, the district president, attended the conference. Miraculously we had twenty-three people in attendance.

> We had a wonderful conference today. All the members spoke, and then I played "Claire D'Lune" on the piano and gave a talk, followed by President Hancock. He is really a great speaker, and the people really loved him, and he is as fine a man as I have ever met. Today he talked about the presidents of the Church, and he really talked from experience about all of them. He knew them all personally except Joseph Smith, Brigham Young, and John Taylor.

After the conference he visited with me for a while and told me he knew this was a difficult place for missionary work but there must be some good people in the town somewhere. He reminded me the prophet Noah preached over a hundred years without getting one convert but that he never quit trying. President Hancock was a great motivator, and I was not offended by what he said but believed it was true.

> SEPTEMBER 13, 1959
>
> When he [President Hancock] got called to come here to this mission, he felt very inadequate because it had been about thirty years since he had spoken any Spanish. However, after talking to David O. McKay

he accepted and came down. After being down here a month or so, he was quite discouraged and felt at a loss as to what to do. That night in a dream he and President McKay were walking arm in arm down a beautiful lane and President McKay told him not to worry about a thing, that he would be able to do everything well and that he would be blessed for doing it. Well, he woke up and since then everything has gone really well. He said he knows it was from God, and it really has helped him.

I was speaking in Sunday School the other morning, and one of the investigators, an Indian girl, said that as I was speaking a white cloud came down from heaven and covered me completely, all except the black Bible I was using. She said that the same cloudlike substance fell on my companion that was sitting by my side. No one else saw it, but this Indian girl swears that it happened, and it has surely strengthened her faith and testimony. God works in a mysterious way His wonders to perform.

SEPTEMBER 20, 1959

Today I had the best meal since I've been here and probably one of the best that I have had in my life. Do you know about the Pan-American Highway that goes from Alaska clear to the tip of South America? Well, it goes right by Tecpan, and they are just completing it. The chief engineer of the job is a Mormon named Hunsaker. They have their camp just outside of Tecpan. Today he came to town and took us out to his camp to eat dinner. Boy, what a dinner! We started off with split pea soup, homemade bread, peanut butter and jam, and real butter. Then came the steaks. I'll swear that the steak I got was three inches thick, and it looked like half the cow—huge! I wish I could have gotten a picture of it. Then there was corn on the cob, french-fried potatoes, all kinds of vegetables, cream puffs, ice cream, and cookies. Boy, I am still full. I can hardly walk, and my companion ate me under the table. He can eat more than anyone that I have ever seen. He is about six feet three inches tall and all stomach.

A theme that seems to run through my letters while I was in Tecpan is how difficult the work was. Even now, forty years later, I can still remember that it was hard and discouraging.

SEPTEMBER 20, 1959

We had kind of a tough week here last week. We worked 61 hours and had only 17 cottage meetings. The mission average for cottage meetings is about 40 each week. So you see that it is tough getting in the doors here. I love the people, but, boy, they are stubborn sometimes.

On September 26, 1959, I turned twenty-one years old. My companion, Elder Reeves, had turned twenty-one on September 23. For birthday presents I gave him a thirty-cent loaf of bread, and on my birthday he got me one as well. It was kind of a corn bread and was very sweet and good. Later that week one of the first converts of the Church in Patzicia, a man named Juan Mich, passed away at age forty-five. He looked a great deal like a man twenty years older than that. Life was hard for these Indian people, and I doubt their life expectancy was very high. All of the elders in the Chimaltenango district attended the funeral, and six of us were pallbearers. Being a pallbearer in Guatemala is no small job. The six of us carried the coffin through the streets of the little town and into the cemetery. The elders had conducted a beautiful funeral service before we led the procession of mourners to the graveyard. His family had already dug the grave. After the coffin had been lowered into this grave, one of his brothers grabbed a shovel and with no ceremony began to shovel the dirt onto the coffin. There was weeping, and had his family not been members of the Church, there would have been horrible wailing as well. These people were well acquainted with death. I am sure that there was not a family in the branch that had not lost many loved ones during their lifetimes. Because of this, the gospel gave them all so much hope that they otherwise would not have had.

OCTOBER 4, 1959

Today is the big celebration of Tecpan. It started Thursday, and today is the big finish. The town has been full of people for a week now, and it has been kind of tough on the missionaries and their work. Everybody has been out in the street, and nobody has been inside. Friday we went to Guatemala City to shop, eat, and see the doctor. My companion has a double hernia, one on each side. He doesn't know when he ruptured himself (I believe it was at the funeral in Patzicia), but one night I just noticed that he was bulging. The doctor thought it would be a good idea to operate on him now while they are still small. We talked to the mission president's wife, Sister Hancock, because the president wasn't in the city and she is going to tell the president and then he will write us a letter letting us know what to do. Maybe I will have a new companion in a few days. He isn't in any pain, and the hernias do not bother him, but I would suggest that he get it taken care of as quickly as possible.

During this trip to Guatemala City (which was always a treat coming in from the mountains), my companion and I went to the movie *The Ten Commandments*. I had seen it before coming on my mission, but I enjoyed it more in the mission field than I ever had before. Guatemala City is probably not as great as it seemed at the time, but to a guy coming in from the outer limits of civilization it seemed as refreshing as an oasis in the Sahara Desert.

Quoting once again from the October 4 letter, I made further comments about the great celebration in Tecpan. This was an annual affair; each city and town in Guatemala had a patron saint, and every year on the birthday of that saint the town would pull out all the stops in celebration.

> They have really been having a fiesta here in Tecpan. I've never seen anything like it before. In this little old town they have a ferris wheel, merry-go-round, and all the carnival games that you can think of. There is also lots of vino (wine). Last night they had about four dances going, and the wine was flowing like water. There are a lot of sick Indians in town today. When they get drunk, they really do a good job of it. This morning was the first time that the mayor was out on the street before us (he stayed up all night).

The inhabitants of Tecpan were no different from most Indians in terms of the effect alcohol had upon them. It was not uncommon at any time to find a man lying in the gutter with flies crawling all over him. It was so common, in fact, that nobody seemed to notice them. I suppose their friends and relatives just figured that they would eventually wake up and come home. How their lives would have been blessed if they just could have accepted the Word of Wisdom. Those who did were blessed beyond measure in that culture.

> OCTOBER 11, 1959
>
> It is Sunday again, and we had a nice Sunday School. Some members came up from Guatemala City to visit in Tecpan, and they visited the Sunday School. I taught the class, and it really seemed strange teaching educated people. I've been teaching simple Indians for so long that my lessons are geared for their understanding, and I'm afraid that the people from Guatemala City got a little bored. Someday I'll get to work among the educated, and it will be good for me. I really love these people here though. They are so much like little children in their understanding. You have to make a big

> story of everything, and just really simple. I imagine that within two weeks I'll be leaving Tecpan. I don't know for sure yet, but I'm positive I'll be leaving the country.
>
> The festival titular of Tecpan ended today, thank goodness. Our prize investigator, Manuel Juarez, got drunk Tuesday night, and now we can't baptize him. We were going to baptize him the 13th, but now it's off. This is the second time we have had him ready and he has gotten drunk both times just two or three days before his baptism. Boy, the old devil is working overtime in this town. Manuel Juarez is a great guy, smart, and will get baptized someday. He is just a little too weak where alcohol is concerned. Also Sister Serech, our Lamanite member, got drunk, and we've been getting her rehabilitated. These darned people just can't resist alcohol down here. You can buy it, wine, just like pop, ten cents a glass, ten cents for a shot of whiskey that is strong enough to burn your stomach out, so for thirty or forty cents you can really hang one on. Everybody has; every man and his dog has been drunk during this two-week celebration. Maybe things will be better now that the festival is over.

I am sure now looking back on these people's addiction to alcohol that for them it was the only way they could escape from the bitter reality of their lives. It wasn't that they were not converted, but in the struggle for survival their addiction to alcohol just got the best of many of them. The culture was built around drinking alcohol. Giving it up to begin a new lifestyle was not easy. Even the little children could buy alcohol without restraint. During the festival I can remember how pained I was when they turned the local schoolhouse into a bar for the two weeks of the celebration. I am sure the adversary gloried in the ignorance of these choice descendants of Father Lehi. He had held them in bondage for many generations and was doing everything in his power to keep them from "arising and shining forth" as the gospel became a part of their lives and transformed them into the mighty and good people it was their destiny to become. As the Savior had told their ancient fathers, these people too were "the children of the prophets." It was their birthright to receive all of the blessings promised to Abraham, Isaac, and Jacob. However, these blessings could only be secured by entering into the new and everlasting covenant. As young missionaries, we often lost sight of what we were attempting to do. Little did we realize that we were in hand-to-hand combat with the evil one. I can't express how I have felt as I have observed the growth of the Church among these people in Guatemala during the past forty years. I have seen scriptural prophecy fulfilled in my lifetime, and I believe that we have only seen the tip of the iceberg regarding what will happen among these children of Lehi.

Approximately twenty years after I left Guatemala, the country experienced a devastating earthquake in which the town of Tecpan was totally leveled. I am not sure how many were killed, but the town was devastated. I am not saying that the wrath of God was visited upon them, but God does work in a mysterious way His wonders to perform. I understand that the town has now been rebuilt and that a small, lovely Latter-day Saint chapel is an important part of the new Tecpan.

> OCTOBER 18, 1959
>
> I imagine that this is my last Sunday in Tecpan. If it is I'll be writing to you from a new place next week. I have now been here five months and one week. A very long five months. I have developed a lot of good habits up here, like going to bed every night at 10:00 and getting up at 5 am each day, Sunday included; working ten hours a day, and studying four hours. I have really learned a lot. I do not know yet one-third of what I want to know about the gospel. I could just kick myself that I watched television instead of studying. That thing is a man killer. It's a good thing once in a while, but it easily can become a vice. I would like to tell you something I read the other day, "Work for the blessings you pray for, and pray only for the blessings you work for." I think if we do this we'll always have everything we need.

In my first few days in Tecpan, I had an experience I apparently never wrote about in one of my letters. One day my companion and I were walking down the street and on the corner was a large group of Indian men. Their native dress looked like pajamas to me. They had on matching shirts and pants that had many bright colors woven into them. As we walked by them, we said hello and continued down the street. We hadn't gone far when something hit me very hard in the back and knocked me to my knees. One of the Indians had thrown a large dirt clod at me, and he really connected. Following my "natural man" instincts, I jumped to my feet and, screaming, began to chase him with all my might. He was running faster than I was, and after about half a block I came to my senses and realized that this was not the image that should be portrayed by a disciple of the Savior. Had I caught him, it's possible he may have killed me. It was just another lesson in learning patience and also a reality check as to how the people felt about the missionaries in that little village.

I had expected to be transferred, but Elder Reeves had to go to Guatemala City to get his hernia operation. A new senior companion had been assigned to take my place, but as I was so well acquainted with Tecpan, President Hancock decided to leave me there with a new companion, Elder William McDonald, until Elder Reeves recovered his health. I was disappointed but decided to make the best of it and was determined to work as hard as I could in Tecpan until the transfer came through. A mission-wide conference was planned for November 15 with Elder Harold B. Lee of the Quorum of the Twelve. I thought that I would not be transferred until that time.

OCTOBER 25, 1959

It is still raining a little every day, but not like before. It rained eight days without stopping, and according to the people that is a lot of rain even for Tecpan. I have been in the mission almost a year now and am really getting started to get the real meaning of missionary work. You have got to have a lot of courage and, at times, plain old gall. You have to be very forward and really try to get into these people's homes so you can tell them how to be saved. And then you have to gain the confidence of the people by living the gospel as well as you can. Well, anyway, it's a really great work and the best thing in the world for anyone.

NOVEMBER 1, 1959

Today is my last day in Tecpan. I leave Wednesday early in the morning. It surely has been a wonderful week. We got 35 cottage meetings, and usually we only get 15 or 18. The Lord has surely blessed us this week. Also to our Wednesday night meeting came 14 investigators. I believe that Tecpan is really starting to open up, and there will be some baptisms soon. About five months ago I tracted out a man, Hermano Galindo, and ever since the first visit I have known that if the Lord would help me, we would baptize that man. He is a Baptist, his daughter is a missionary, and his son is a preacher in the Baptist Church. At first he had some doubts as to whether this church is the true and only church in which we can gain salvation, but the Lord manifested His Spirit through me to him, and finally he has gained a testimony. Every time I have ever visited him, I have been inspired from

> on high to talk in such a way as to convince this old man. He is 65 years old, and he knows that I have been telling him the truth. His family will not let him come to meeting, or wouldn't, but yesterday we had a wonderful visit with him, he had tears in his eyes when we finished, and he said that he was coming to church today even if his family tried to kill him. He came, and he will keep coming. He will be baptized. I won't see it, but I know he will be baptized.
>
> I will be sad and glad to leave Tecpan all at the same time. I learned the greatest lesson of my mission up here this last week, that if an elder will dedicate himself 100 percent to the missionary work and not think of anything else, the Lord will help him to bring souls into the Church. I have learned that one thing in such a forceful way that it will remain with me the rest of my life and the rest of my mission. The Lord always helps if we do our part, as He says, "I the Lord am bound when ye do what I say, but when ye do not what I say ye have no promise." It is the truth too.

At the time I wrote this letter I did not know where I was being transferred. I was simply told to come to the mission office in Guatemala City and I would then receive my new assignment. This was the end of not only a significant time in my mission but also a significant time of preparation for the remainder of my life. I am grateful that I had a Tecpan experience as a twenty-year-old. I learned to deal with adversity, and the lessons I learned at that time blessed me throughout the remainder of my mission and throughout my life, especially helping me to deal with being paralyzed and on life support. I see the hand of the Lord in the various assignments that were given me as a missionary. Reflecting back I can see how, for me, the assignments I had were inspired. Each one gave me the experience I would need, along with the spiritual depth that was being developed, to bless me throughout my life. Although I didn't realize it at the time, what was happening to me is best expressed in the words of Francis Webster. He, along with his wife and little baby, experienced the hardship and suffering visited upon the Martin Handcart Company. He was only twenty-six years old at that time. Later in life, as an old man responding to some criticism regarding the wisdom of sending the handcart companies out so late in the year, he said, "We suffered beyond anything you can imagine. However, those who survived came through with the absolute knowledge that God lives, for we became acquainted with him in our extremities." In retrospect I believe this statement accurately describes the greatest lesson learned from the first year of my mission, although mine was small compared to that of the handcart pioneers. Adversity can be a blessing that enables us to become acquainted with God. I think this is one of the great by-products that come to young men serving in the mission field.

CHAPTER 8

# *Ahuachapan*

President Hancock was inspired to send me to El Salvador. I boarded a plane in Guatemala City and flew the short distance to El Salvador. I landed in San Salvador, the capital city. Unfortunately, the entire time I was there, I did not know that my grandfather Frederick Rushton spent about a year of his life as a bricklayer in that country. Had I known that, it would have made my stay in that country even more special than it was.

To my eyes coming from Tecpan, San Salvador was the biggest and most beautiful city on earth. The people were intelligent, warm, and friendly, but the city was busy too. I was almost run over several times and was only saved from certain death by having an alert missionary companion pull me out of harm's way and back onto the sidewalk.

The branch had over a hundred members with an average attendance of around 95. It was a wonderful experience to meet with these great Latter-day Saints. Everyone was very excited about the visit of Harold B. Lee on November 13, 1959. The choir in our branch was to sing at the conference, and I was asked to lead it. I never dreamed when I was taking choir-conducting classes at BYU that I would be leading a choir in El Salvador that would be singing for an apostle of the Lord who would one day be the prophet of this Church. It was an exciting time.

> NOVEMBER 15, 1959
>
> We just had a wonderful conference with Harold B. Lee and his wife. It was really wonderful. One of the greatest experiences that I have ever had was talking to this servant of God. I learned many things from him about the missionary work and about being a man. I hope that I can put into practice all that I learned from him.

Forty years later I can still remember how impressed I was with Harold B. Lee. He was easy to talk to and seemed like an Idaho farmer who had just come to town to visit with us. I knew that I was in the presence of greatness, yet he was so personable and friendly that I never felt uncomfortable with him. He had a personal interview with each of us, and when we were through I felt good about myself and about the work I had been sent to do in the land of the Lamanites. I knew he was a true servant of the Lord. My testimony was strengthened regarding the fact that prophets, seers, and revelators are on the earth today.

I was in San Salvador only a short time before being transferred to Ahuachapan. Late one afternoon several of the missionaries thought we should attend the new movie that had just been released entitled *Ben Hur.* It was not against mission policy to attend an occasional movie, and I had attended the movie theater only twice in the year I had been in Central America. We went, and as you might imagine, we were thrilled with this epic movie. We arrived home quite late, and as we walked into our apartment our district leader was waiting for us. For some reason I have never been so embarrassed in my life. He asked us where we had been, and one of the elders told him we had been at the movies. I could not look him in the eyes, and my face was red with embarrassment. I doubt I could have looked guiltier if I had committed some horrible sin. Here I was, sent to Central America to bring souls unto Christ, and I had been wasting my time at the movies.

Shortly after this episode President Hancock put me on a bus and sent me to Ahuachapan to be the branch president. His parting words through the open windows as the bus rolled away were, "Elder Rushton, are you good at solving problems?" With his ominous words ringing in my ears, I wondered what awaited me in my next assignment.

My new companion in Ahuachapan was a native named Cesar Sanchez. He didn't speak any English, and because of this my command of the Spanish language took a quantum leap forward.

> Well, I'm getting a little bit accustomed to the country of El Salvador now after the little time that I've been here. It is really different from Guatemala. It is the richest country in Central America and one of the richest in the world. The reason is because it grows coffee, nothing but coffee; all you can see for miles and miles is coffee. Ahuachapan is one of the richest towns in El Salvador. The big plantation owners live here, and it is really a beautiful town. It has a population of about 15,000 people, and compared to Tecpan's 1,500 this is quite a change. It is easy to get visits, and everybody will talk with you, and that is really something. The branch has about 40 members and is just full of problems. A couple of members have committed fornication and will be excommunicated, and we have all kinds of apostate members, and, believe me, there is nothing worse than an apostate member. I hope that we can find some good honest people here that will accept the gospel.

In my innocence, and having come from the mountains of Guatemala, I probably thought that El Salvador was the richest country in Central America and in the world. I am sure that was not the case, but it seemed that way to me. It was true, however, that Ahuachapan was one of the richest towns in El Salvador. There was no middle-class in Ahuachapan. There were the very rich and the very poor. The rich plantation owners had beautiful homes with glimmering tile floors and servants to take care of every need. The poor lived in homes not much better than those of the people in Tecpan. I had never seen such a disparity between the rich and the poor as I did in Ahuachapan. I am no student of political science, but I can understand why there was a great civil war that broke out in that country not too many years after I had finished my mission. Thousands were brutally murdered, and many members of the Church suffered, as well as the missionary work, for a lengthy period.

> Our branch here in Ahuachapan has 43 members, and it is full of problems. They really had a big mess here about a month ago, and it is my job to get everybody happy and get them to loving the gospel and the Church. I haven't time to tell you what happened, but the branch is divided: one-half sticks together, and the other half sticks together. My

> job is to be right in the middle, making everybody think I'm his best buddy and not taking sides. Needless to say it is tough, the toughest job I have ever tackled.
>
> Last night one of the women members came up to me after sacrament meeting and wanted to talk to me, so we went into the branch president's office and talked. She was crying and was really sad about the branch and the bad feelings that are here, so we talked and talked, two and a half hours, and when she left she was smiling and happy. The Lord has really helped me so far in this branch. Being branch president here in these countries is like being baby-sitter to 43 separate problems. These people have so much to overcome—the influence of the Catholic Church and their own natural state of being irresponsible. It is hard for them to accept responsibility; however, from time to time you really find a great person, one you can trust, and that is a find here.

I doubt these people were naturally irresponsible, and I attribute these words to the frustration of a young missionary. Little did I know at the time, but there would be numerous times in my life when I would be in offices counseling with people who had severe problems. What an incredible training ground my mission was for the positions of responsibility I held later in my life. Most missions are different today, but in El Salvador in 1959 the young missionaries not only did missionary work but were also heavily involved in Church leadership and administration. This branch was torn apart, and I began to discover at that time that I had an ability to get along with others. I could influence them to remain active in the Church while ridding themselves of offended feelings and the grudges they carried. However, the entire time I was in Ahuachapan I felt like I was walking on eggshells.

Ahuachapan was enjoyable. It was hot and humid, but the countryside was green and lush. We had plenty of investigators, and my hopes ran high for many baptisms. I soon discovered that one problem in Ahuachapan was that many of the people were addicted to coffee. This was only natural because of all of the coffee plantations that surrounded the city and created its economy. It took great faith for the people to give up their coffee and live the Word of Wisdom. Drinking coffee was also an important social practice and was very much a part of every meal and every gathering, both within and without the home.

As I mentioned earlier, Elder Cesar Sanchez was my companion during the first month or so in Ahuachapan. He had a wonderful personality, and we got along extremely well. He did not speak a word of English, which was good for me in terms of getting more fluent in Spanish. We would buy a newspaper every week and would read it together. He helped me to understand the words and phrases that were unfamiliar. I especially enjoyed reading the comic strips in Spanish with him. As always, I was saddened when I heard that I was to have a new companion. He was Elder Gary Berglund, who was very enthusiastic and fun to work with.

As Christmas approached, we found a Christmas tree, which was a dead bush we painted white. Some members gave us a string of lights, and, strangely enough, it made it seem like Christmas. In an attempt to placate both factions of the branch, we accepted two separate invitations to eat dinner on Christmas Eve. Christmas Eve is the highlight of the Christmas season in El Salvador. Both dinners we attended were magnificent affairs. These members didn't have much, but no expense was spared in entertaining the missionaries. The entire branch was pleased with us, but I thought I would be sick because of how much I had eaten as a peace offering to appease the restless natives. We had just crawled into bed with visions of tortillas and beans dancing in our heads, when suddenly it seemed that war had broken out in Ahuachapan. We lived near the Catholic cathedral, and as was the custom at midnight on Christmas Eve they shot rocket after rocket into the sky. They exploded with a deafening roar, welcoming in the birthday of the Prince of Peace.

On Christmas Day my companion and I took a bus to San Salvador to participate in a missionary conference. There were fourteen of us in attendance, and we had a wonderful meeting, which was a unique way for me to celebrate Christmas—it was the best way. This was my second Christmas in the mission field. We sang Christmas carols and bore our testimonies and felt the spirit of the Christ. I did not miss the traditional celebration of receiving and opening a multitude of presents.

My parents sent me a sweater, and my brother Kim sent me a tie. I wrote:

> I am not an undertaker; you can send ties that are a little louder, stripes, designs, etc. I could sure use a couple more ties.
>
> I appreciate all that you have done and are doing for me. I realize how tough it is for you, and it really makes me happy to know that everybody is still behind me. A person's family is the most important thing in the world, as you all know. We had to sleep in San Salvador overnight. Because we didn't have any place to stay, we slept on the benches in the chapel—a tough night, because the benches had slats.

> Needless to say, we didn't sleep very long, and all in all it was a very happy Christmas.

The first week of January 1960, the district president, another missionary, came to our meetings on Sunday. We spent a busy afternoon and evening visiting with problem members and then riding horses out into the countryside to visit a special member family that lived on a little farm. They were perhaps the finest family I had met thus far in my mission. Riding the horses was always enjoyable, but two hours of riding in that tropical heat with the sun beating down on us took its toll.

> It is the end of the year, and I have had a million records that I have to turn in. It is really good experience being branch president, just like being bishop of a ward. I have to keep the financial records, the tithing, etc., and I believe that my arithmetic has really come along pretty well. If you know of any way to improve your mathematics, tell me.

Ahuachapan was another great learning experience for me. The first two months I was there, I learned many things, especially about people. The branch wasn't growing as fast as it should because of gossip and fights between members. It was impressed on my mind then and since how devastating gossip and backbiting can be on the spirits of those who engage in it. It can be poisonous to the spirit of a family or an organization like the Church. In a little branch like the one we had in Ahuachapan, it was devastating.

One of the highlights of serving in Ahuachapan was getting to know a family by the name of Nicia. Every other week we would ride horses out into the countryside to visit these marvelous people. I have already mentioned one such excursion. Brother and Sister Nicia had seven children. I had never met such a close family. They worked together, prayed together, and went to church together. We always felt a beautiful spirit in their humble home, which was a grass hut. They lived four miles outside of town, and each Sunday, starting very early in the morning, they would walk to church. In the six months I was there I cannot recall them ever missing church on a Sunday. Only one of the children could read—the mother and father could not—and so each evening after the work was done, the family would gather together around a single candle while a young boy read out loud from the Book of Mormon. Because of this daily reading of the scriptures, the entire family was gaining a great knowledge of the gospel. The unmistakable peace and warmth of the Spirit was also evident in this most humble of homes. None of them

*Nicia family and Elder Rushton, Ahuachapan.*

owned a pair of shoes, and their clothes, though clean, were very raggedy. One of the sweetest and most humbling experiences of my mission or my life was to have Brother Nicia seek me out before sacrament meeting each Sunday and give me his tithing. The tithing could not have amounted to more than just a few cents, but it was an honest tithing—much like the widow's mite. I couldn't fully appreciate, then or now, what a sacrifice this must have been for such a poverty-stricken family. I vowed then that if the Lord would ever permit me to earn any money during my lifetime that I would be honest in paying my tithing. Not doing so would have made me an incredible hypocrite, having accepted the tithing of this humble man and his family as their branch president.

JANUARY 24, 1960

I just got back about 10 minutes ago from Chalchuapa, where Elder Berglund, my companion, and I go once a month to speak in church. It is a 45-minute ride from Ahuachapan, and is very pretty. I'm really starting to get into the swing of things here in Ahuachapan, and I like it here better than in any place in which I have been. I have been here now almost two and a half months; how the time flies. In a few days I will have fulfilled one-half of my mission, and it just doesn't seem possible.

*Elder Sellers and Elder Rushton.*

Elder Berglund was given a transfer, and I received a new challenge in the form of Elder Sellers. Elder Sellers had been in the mission two months and had been very sick physically and was also suffering from a severe case of homesickness. He wouldn't work and had not been able to get along with any of his previous companions, so President Hancock sent him to Ahuachapan as my companion. President Hancock knew that I had been able to get along with all of my companions, and he was hoping that I could help Elder Sellers. Thankfully I really liked him, and he eventually began to get into the spirit of his mission. I don't say this in a bragging sort of way, but truthfully one of the gifts I have been blessed with is to get along with others. This began to manifest itself in the mission field. This gift was a blessing to me as I served as a bishop and a stake president.

FEBRUARY 1, 1960

We have a big mess in the branch. Some time back two members committed fornication, and the young girl had an illegitimate child. Down here that isn't anything, but because they were Mormons it really got the people talking. Well, the girl was given full membership because she had repented fully. The boy was suspended, which means he cannot do anything in the Church. The other day the boy hit the girl and tore her dress, and a bunch of people saw it, so she abandoned the child and took off. We do not know where she is. We have the child in the home of its grandmother, and she is taking care of her while we try to find out where her daughter is. The father of the child does not want it either, and it really makes me sad to see the poor little baby right in the mess without a friend. We blessed the child in sacrament meeting last January, but we couldn't give it a last name. Things like this really make me sick. However, I'm sure everything will work out all right.

I really love the missionary work, I love the people and I have just had to grow up fast to be able to carry all the responsibility that I have. I love being branch president. It is really a big challenge—like being bishop, with less work, of course. I pray that I can continue to progress and help these people to live clean lives so that they can gain their salvation one day and so they can be truly happy. Happiness comes from

> doing the Lord's will and in no other way. All other happiness is passing happiness, and to be happy forever we need the Lord on our side.

Elder Sellers and I took a bus into San Salvador to look for typewriters. We each wanted one and felt that in the capital we would be able to find a good deal. A typewriter was such a valuable tool for working as the branch president and in writing letters and communicating with others. We searched all day but could not find the right deal for the right kind of typewriter to meet our needs. Just as we were about to catch the bus back to Ahuachapan we went into a pawn shop, and there sitting on a shelf were two typewriters. They were just what we had been looking for. I bought a year-old Remington Quiet Riter, a portable, for $38. New, it would have cost $200. I used this machine for the rest of my mission and also during a big part of my undergraduate work at BYU.

While serving in Ahuachapan, I had an interesting experience with the Spanish language. One of our investigators complimented me one day on how good my Spanish was. He said, however, that it was textbook Spanish and if I would learn some of the idiomatic expressions used by the people, then they would more readily accept me. He proceeded to write down about twenty words on a sheet of paper with a brief explanation after each word as to the context in which it would be appropriate to use it. In my innocence I memorized all twenty words and knew exactly when to use them. We were then teaching a lady, a widow, who had several young children. She had been taught by a number of missionaries before my companion and I met her. As we were giving her and her children a discussion, I perceived an opportunity to use one of the words I had learned. I said, "The teachings of the Catholic Church are ——!" I had no sooner said the word than the children started laughing hysterically and rolling on the floor. The mother's face turned bright red, and she said, "I have heard that word many times, but I never thought I would hear it from the lips of a Mormon elder." There have been few times in my life that I have been so embarrassed. We claimed ignorance of what I had said, and she must have forgiven us, evidenced by her subsequent baptism. We went directly from her house to the home of one of the stalwart members of the branch. We had him read the words and tell us which ones were appropriate to use. As he looked at the list, his face went bright red as well. As he looked at each word, he would say, "Never, never use this word!" I guess the investigator had given me twenty of the most vile swear words in the Spanish language.

Before I had memorized those words, I never heard them. After learning them and the context in which they were used, I was painfully aware of hearing them constantly on the streets during the remainder of my mission. Not surprisingly, the young man who gave them to me was never baptized. When I confronted him with the words he had given me, he said that everybody used them and that I shouldn't be so sensitive. It was a learning experience for me.

> FEBRUARY 15, 1960
>
> Yesterday we had a marvelous conference in San Salvador. We took a busload of people from Ahuachapan—about 47. I got to give the opening speech of the conference and present the theme of the quarterly conference, which was, "For behold, this is my work and my glory, to bring to pass the immortality and eternal life of man." It was a wonderful experience, and the Spirit of the Lord was really in the conference as about 250 Lamanite people gathered in the chapel of San Salvador to hear about their salvation and how to gain life eternal. It was the first conference in which I have had the opportunity to speak, and it was really a thrill. I was a little nervous at first, but that all left me as I started talking to those wonderful people.

About this time in my mission I was beginning to truly appreciate the opportunity of being in Central America. Of course I didn't know how missions were in other places in the world, so my perspective was somewhat limited. At the time, however, I couldn't conceive of any other mission offering the missionaries a greater challenge just in terms of culture and living conditions.

> I am so thankful that I am here in Central America. I could never express in words my thankfulness. Living in Central America just isn't really pleasant all of the time. The people really live in poverty, and we are right here with them, sharing in their problems and trying to help them. For this I am happy. I don't like easy things; you don't get anything from doing things that are easy to do. This mission is a challenge every day, and it is not easy at all, and for that I love it. It is no place for a sissy. There are many that come down that get so discouraged that they want to go home. It's no place for a loafer either, and if a person can come down here and work hard and love the people and forget about himself, he wouldn't trade this place for anyplace in the world.

Actually, our living conditions in Ahuachapan were very good. We hired a woman named Berta De Maldonado to work for us. She was basically deaf, overweight, and not beautiful to look at, but she had one of the greatest spirits of anyone I have ever met. She would come early in the morning and cook all of our meals, make our beds, wash our clothes, and shop for food because we had no refrigerator. She basically mothered us. We sensed immediately that she truly liked us and worried about our welfare. We taught her how to make pancakes and hamburgers. When she combined that with her expertise in cooking fried bananas, beans and rice, and wonderful corn tortillas, I put on ten pounds. We would leave literature about the Church in conspicuous places around the apartment. Almost daily we would find her engrossed in reading these missionary tracts. She would suddenly look up, see us, and get the most embarrassed look imaginable on her face. I suggested one day that we teach her the missionary discussions and she enthusiastically accepted the offer. We chose to teach her in the chapel, which was on the busiest street in Ahuachapan. We set up a blackboard, opened all the windows, and taught her the gospel in our loudest voices—partly because she was practically deaf and partly to attract more investigators. As we taught her, twenty or thirty people would stand at the windows and listen to what we were saying. Berta and her young son sat on the front bench, smiling and taking it all in. It turned out that she was a voracious reader and soon was completing her reading of the Book of Mormon. She began attending church regularly and was always a joy to be around in spite of her hearing problem. She was not quite ready for baptism when I was transferred from Ahuachapan, but just a few days after my arrival at my new assignment, I received a precious letter from her. She had just been baptized and wrote, "Elder Rushton, I used to be your maid, but now I am your sister!" Her baptism was reason enough for me to have been sent to Ahuachapan. In 2002, the missionary who replaced me in Ahuachapan, Eugene Romney, sent me an email indicating that Berta De Maldonado had been faithful all these years and that her son had served a mission. He also reported to me that our little branch of forty-eight had grown into a stake of Zion, the El Salvador Ahuachapan Stake.

FEBRUARY 22, 1960

It's really starting to get hot here, and they tell me that the hottest months are the months of March, April, and May. After this comes the rain. It rains just about every day for all of the months of July, August, and September. I have been here in Ahuachapan about three and a half months now, and I have really been putting on the weight. We really

> eat like kings, and our old maid really babies us. She looks like a football player but is worth her weight in gold. I have never met a person that I have liked any better than her in all of my life.
>
> The other day we had a funeral here in the city. One of the member's little girls died, and we had to bury her. The little baby that died was 19 months old and died of the measles. Anyway they said it was the measles. I kind of think it was because of the dirt. It was really a strange thing, and I'll have to tell it to you. We were walking down the road toward the country when all of a sudden this member lady walked out to the side of the road and invited us in. We walked into the house, and I noticed that they had an old wooden box on a table and that they were pasting white paper on it. I asked them what it was and the woman told me that it was a coffin. Then she told me, just as though it happened every day that her daughter had died the night before. They didn't seem to be shaken about it at all. The baby had been sick for a couple of days, and then all of a sudden it died, just like that. Anyway they finished the box while we were standing there, put the baby inside, nailed down the lid, and we headed for the cemetery. When we got there, the hole had been dug, so the father of the baby jumped down into the hole and somebody handed him the box with the baby. He climbed out, grabbed a shovel, and started tossing in the dirt. Afterward they did cry a little bit, but very little, and the reason is that they are so used to death. Every day you see a funeral procession in the street and especially funerals for the children. These people live with death constantly, and a death, even though it hurts, is no big thing.

I wonder now if what I said about the feelings of these people in having their baby die was true. I think that they were very stoic people, well acquainted with adversity, but now I am sure that this death hurt them badly. Having children and grandchildren of my own helps me to realize what these people were going through in their struggle to survive.

I discovered that alcohol consumption was as big a problem in El Salvador as it was in Guatemala. While I was in Ahuachapan, the first week of March of 1960, the Catholic Church sponsored a celebration called the Sweet Name of Jesus. They had a carnival complete with all of the carnival rides, but the main attraction was the beer and wine that was made available to even the poorest of the poor. They had a little train called the Gallo Train. Gallo was the most popular brand of beer in El Salvador. It is comparable to Budweiser in the United States. To ride the train, which didn't run on tracks but through the streets of Ahuachapan, the price of admission was to drink a Gallo beer. The train was crowded every hour of every day the carnival lasted. At night there were fireworks. At least that was really quite spectacular. I never could figure out what this celebration had to do with the Sweet Name of Jesus. We had two major casualties in our little branch because of this Catholic extravaganza. Two of our most stalwart men, who were recovering alcoholics, succumbed to the temptation of the abundance of alcohol and were unconscious for several days. We worked hard to rehabilitate them and eventually helped them to resume full activity in the Church.

I continued to be impressed with the Nicia family that I mentioned earlier. They had been baptized only four months before my arrival in Ahuachapan. I had the privilege of interviewing the father, Ernesto, and his two oldest sons, Alfonso and Adolfo, to receive the priesthood. It was my opportunity and a great blessing to confer the priesthood upon these three humble Lamanites. Their love and commitment to the gospel was demonstrated in many ways. The countrywide conference we had in San Salvador was surely a test of their faith. The bus we had rented to take our people to the conference left at 6:30 AM the day of the conference. In order to catch the bus, the Nicia family left their home at 3:30 AM to walk into town. The family of nine arrived on time, spent the entire day in meetings, returned on the bus at around 9 PM, and walked all the way home, carrying the younger children on their backs, arriving at around midnight. This great family was teaching me an invaluable lesson regarding commitment to the covenants we make with the Lord in the waters of baptism. What a joy to have known these simple, humble, and faithful sons and daughters of God. They have influenced my desire to serve the Lord and to make whatever sacrifice has been necessary to fulfill and magnify the assignments that have come to me over the past forty years.

MARCH 6, 1960

Ever since I have been here in Ahuachapan I have been looking for a new house and chapel. The one we have is just too big, and what is more we have to pay $120 a month in rent, which is outrageous here in this country. The owners of the house where we now are living are the richest people in town. Boy, they have the biggest house I have ever seen; the living room is so big that you could play basketball in it, and I am not kidding. They own a lot of coffee farms, and I would say that they are close to millionaires. I really like them however, and they are quite kind. They have a nice piano in the house, so every

> once in a while when we are in the neighborhood we drop in and I play them a few pieces on their piano. They really enjoy it, and I do too. Well, the other day we found a house that will be just perfect for our chapel, and I'm sure that we are going to move. These people found out about it and sent their maid down to get us. When we got to their big old house, they had some ice cream ready for us and also gave a great big bottle of honey to us. Then they really started talking turkey, telling us not to move because we had the best house in town and telling us that the house where we are going to move isn't any good and that the people that own the house are crooks, etc. It was really funny, and now I know why they are millionaires. Also, I was thinking that those people who were so rich didn't know, in fact didn't even have any idea at all why they were here in this earth. As we were talking to the señora of the house, who has traveled in Europe, England, Australia, Mexico, and all over the world, I asked her if she really knew what the purpose of this life is. It really stumped her. All of her life she had never once asked herself that question. She has spent all of her time having a good time and has done a good job at it. But she had to admit that as far as having any purpose in life, or in the hereafter, she just didn't. Then I thought of the words of Christ when He said that he that had eternal life was rich, and he that didn't have eternal life, even though he was rich, would be poor. And this smart woman understood it also, because even with all of her wealth she isn't completely happy nor will she be happy unless she one day understands the gospel of Christ.
>
> Also, I found a 13-year-old kid here in this town who can play the piano better than I can. The people whom we are thinking of renting from, have a piano also, and the señora told me that her son played. Saturday we went to their house to get the key to the other house. She invited me and I started playing the Revolutionary Etude by Chopin. Well, she really liked it and also some jerky-looking little kid who was sitting there. When I got done she told me that the jerky-looking kid was her son that played the piano, so I asked him to sit down and play something. I thought he would probably play chopsticks or something, but he started out on the Minute Waltz by Chopin, and I'll bet he played it in 50 seconds. Boy those little old fingers were really flying, and I was so amazed that I couldn't clap. I didn't even think that anybody in the whole town knew who Chopin was.

Being able to play the piano was a great blessing during my mission. The piano in the Ahuachapan chapel was in terrible shape. Hardly any of the keys from middle C upward worked, and I was reduced to playing the hymns on the lower half of the keyboard. I believe that is why I enjoyed going into these wealthy homes and playing a decent piano. A mission is an incredible thing. Here was this boy from Ruth, Nevada, walking into a mansion, telling the lady of the house that she didn't understand the meaning of life, and then sitting down at the piano in another mansion and playing a little Chopin. How improbable is that?

> March 28, 1960
>
> We have really been working hard with our investigators and will be ready for some baptisms in the month of April (or first of May). All of the people that we have ready are really good people, and even though some are old reformed drunks, they really have testimonies. For example, we have Brother Antonio Chiquila, who is about 30 years old and is really working hard. We have had trouble with him, because every time that we get him all ready, his friends tempt him too much and he drinks a couple of beers. We've really got him going this time, and with the help of the Lord we will baptize him. Also, the family of Hector Sea is just about ready. The sister was working on Sunday, but she quit now and they will be baptized. We have lots of good people going, and with a lot of prayer and work they one day will be members.
>
> We just reorganized the branch Sunday, setting apart Catalina de Lima as the Primary president, Luis Angel Figueroa as superintendent of the Sunday School, and Reynaldo Padilla, and Rolando Valiente as the two counselors. The branch is more united now, and I'm sure that with the help of every member and with the inspiration of God that this town is really going to prosper and grow.
>
> I'm learning new things every day and discovering new talents all of the time also. However, I am losing some of the old ones and sure wish I had a little time to practice the piano. But there is a time for everything, and right now I've got time for just one thing, and that's the work of the Lord. It is a wonderful work, and I love it. Wish that everyone could be a missionary one day. You gain so much because you give so much away.

It was during this period of time in Ahuachapan that I received news that my Grandmother Jensen had passed away. This was my mother's mother, whom I truly loved and respected. She had lived with us many months out of each year for the last years of her life. I was saddened to receive the news regarding her death, but she had been suffering for a long time, and it was a blessing for her to be released from mortality. She was a great lady in every way. She raised eight children by herself after her husband, Allen LeRoy Young, passed away at an early age. She was very self-sufficient and worked hard to keep her family together. I wish I could have seen her at least one more time, but it was not to be.

While I was in Ahuachapan, the mission president set a goal for the mission of a thousand convert baptisms for 1960. He was inspired to do this because of a talk given by President David O. McKay that a new era in the Church was beginning. President McKay made it abundantly clear that although the Church had grown greatly since its establishment in 1830, the Lord expected much more. It was at this time that he coined the phrase "every member a missionary." Taking this talk to heart, President Hancock let us know that the standard for the Central American Mission was to be one baptism per missionary each month. This would result in a thousand baptisms for 1960. This may not seem like much now, but when you consider that in 1959 in all of Central America there had been only 350 baptisms, this new standard was a quantum leap forward and would test our faith as missionaries as we worked to achieve it.

At the time of this announcement, we had only baptized one person in Ahuachapan while I was there. However, we did have six or seven people who were getting ready for baptism on May 7 and another group of seven or eight that would be ready by June 7.

April 6, 1960

Wednesday we went out to the country with Rolando Valiente and Luis Angel Figueroa. They are the ward teachers of the family (Nicia) that lives in the country. We tried to rent four horses but just got three and one mule. We put Luis Angel on the mule and started. The mule had a terrible bit in its mouth. Luis Angel had never ridden anything before except a bus, and the mule wanted to run, and run it did! It was the funniest thing I have ever seen in my life. Luis Angel was hanging on with all four feet and hollering and hitting the poor old mule. The more he shouted, the more the mule ran, and the mule ran straight through, over, between, along, and under everything that happened to be in its path. When we finally caught Luis Angel and stopped the mule, he got down and said that he was going to walk the rest of the way. He was really scared, and so Elder Sellers, who is an old cowboy from way back, got on the mule, and we finally made it to the house of the member family.

Saturday night, the two oldest boys of the family from the country (Nicia) came to town to help us clean the chapel. Sunday we ordained them all deacons, and it is the priesthood holders' job to clean the chapel. They stayed with us all night here in the chapel, and I have never seen such clean, pure, innocent little kids in all of my life. We had a meeting lined up for Saturday night, but nobody showed up, so we decided to take the two kids to the show. One is 16 and the other 13, and they had never seen a show in all of their lives. We took them in, bought them the best seat in the house, and then just sat there looking at them enjoy that darn old show. They were just amazed. They wouldn't believe that the men were just actors; they thought that it was the real thing. They just sat on the edge of the chairs bug-eyed. Boy, they are really chosen people; they have more faith than any other people I have seen in all my life, bar none. The work is going great, and within a month we should baptize about five people.

### April 10, 1960

Saturday we administered to a little boy that was quite sick, and the next day he was a lot better. The administration really helped him a lot. In about an hour we have to administer to a little girl also. We have an epidemic of flu here and the doctors are few and far between, so the people depend on us to help out. These people have great faith and sometimes make me feel that I don't even know what faith is. I have developed more faith since I have been here in Ahuachapan than at any other time during my mission. I know, and have felt continually the Spirit of the Lord guiding and helping me with a great number of problems that we have had.

### April 25, 1960

I am going to ask that you have a special day of fasting and prayer for the persons that are going to get baptized here so that during the days that remain between now and the seventh none of them will fall into one of the devil's traps. Fast and then pray and tell Father in Heaven why you are fasting, and I am sure that He will hear and help these people here in Ahuachapan. As you know, a missionary has no right on earth to feel proud of himself when a person gets baptized. He should just be happy that the Lord has given the convert His Spirit so that they could recognize the truth when the elders were teaching him.

Saturday we went to San Salvador to talk to President Hancock, and he told me that I wouldn't be here in Ahuachapan for very much more time. We usually stay in a town only about six months, and in a very short time I will have been here six months. He talked like he was

> going to give me a job with a little more responsibility than the job that I now have. I was glad that he was pleased with the job that I have done here in Ahuachapan, but I know that I have made many mistakes. I have learned more in this town than I could have learned in any other town in the mission because of all the troubles we have had.
>
> As you know, I have about one year to go, and my suits look like it. This is the only country in all of Central America where you can buy good American suits, and I could get a good one for $40. I want you to tell me if we can afford it. If not, tell me no, because I can get by if I have to, but it will probably be the last chance I will have to get a good suit. If we can't do it, just tell me, and I want you to tell me the truth too.

Throughout my mission I was very sensitive regarding the amount of money I spent. My mom and dad took a second job as custodians at the elementary school across the street from our home to pay for my mission. My mother would go there each day at noon to sweep and clean the cafeteria. When my dad would get home from work in the evening, they would go together to sweep, mop, and dust the classrooms and clean the restrooms. This would take them two or three or more hours each evening, and in the winter it was also dad's responsibility to keep the

*Elder Rushton and Ahuachapan converts, Rio de Paz, El Salvador.*

furnace functioning correctly, which was an additional burden. If ever I was tempted to spend money or time foolishly, I would picture in my mind my mom and dad working as custodians, and I would immediately repent. I was impressed with the sacrifice they were willing to make to give me the opportunity to serve a mission. As I reflect back over the years, my respect for them and their act of service and sacrifice on my behalf grows and deepens.

MAY 1, 1960

The big day of the baptismal service is drawing near, and the seven people that are to be baptized are really doing fine. I am sure it is because the Lord is really blessing us and the people in this town of Ahuachapan. Yesterday in my investigator class of investigators about 15 people were out, which is a really good-sized class of investigators. We are going to baptize seven more people in June, but I doubt if I will be here to see it. President Hancock told me that I should be leaving Ahuachapan soon after this baptismal service the 7th of May. I will be really sad leaving Ahuachapan because I believe that it is here that I have learned how to be a real missionary. My lessons have gotten much better, and I have learned how to deal with people better than ever before."

MAY 11, 1960

Well, Saturday we baptized seven people in the Rio de Paz, a big river near here, and it was really a great day. The names of those we baptized are Victor Manual Canenguez, Rolando Sea, Hector Sea, Christina de Sea, Rosa Lillian Cortez, Antonio Chiquila, and Edgar Rodriguez. They are all fine people and will be good Mormons. I now have six months in Ahuachapan, and have been here longer than in any other town.

I guess Saturday was one of the biggest days of my life. Just think, we have helped seven people to find their salvation, people who just a few months ago hadn't even heard of Joseph Smith or the Church of Jesus Christ. When we went down to the river, I was thinking of Ammon and his brothers who were among the Lamanites almost 2,000 years ago, and the great joy they received for having helped their brothers to find the truth and throw off the curse that they were living under. I doubt that Ammon could have been much happier than I when I was in the river baptizing those people by the power of the holy priesthood. We are going to baptize four more in June, and maybe a lot more in July, but I won't be here to see it, I am sure.

So ended my work in Ahuachapan. Little did I know that many years later where there was once a tiny struggling branch, there would be a stake of Zion. I, of course, felt sad that I didn't get to baptize those other people we were preparing, especially our maid, but such is the nature of missionary work. It little matters who performs the ordinance. We sow seeds that grow and take root, and sometimes another does the harvesting. The important thing is that the harvest takes place and the sheaves are gathered in.

CHAPTER 9

# Mazatenango

It was very difficult for me to leave Ahuachapan, almost as hard as leaving home. I had grown to love those people with all my heart. On May 17, 1960, I arrived in the city of Mazatenango, Guatemala. Mazatenango was about twenty minutes from Retalhuleu (where I had served approximately one year before), and it was even hotter there than it was in Retalhuleu, which seemed impossible to me. On a clear day I could see the ocean from Mazatenango.

My new calling was to be the branch president and supervising elder of the Mazatenango District. In today's terms, a supervising elder would be a district or zone leader. Once a week I traveled out into the district to work with a set of missionaries. Things were not going well in Mazatenango. They hadn't had a baptism in all of 1960, and my first Sunday in the branch, only one investigator attended. My first impression was that I was facing a great challenge in this new assignment.

MAY 22, 1960

I bought a new suit in San Salvador, wash and wear, so thin you can see through it, and I am really putting it to good use here. I won't have to buy anything else all the rest of my mission—just food.

We are living in the house of members in Mazatenango and have good clean food and a good place to stay. The Lord has blessed me with good health all my mission. I was sick for about two days 14 months ago, and outside of an ingrown toenail and a few good boils and colds I have really been in great shape. Some elders go home from here just about wrecked, and I thank the Lord each day for the good health I have, and have had.

This last statement I made about my good health would prove to be full of irony as you will see as the story unfolds. The time of year I was in Mazatenango it rained every afternoon for two hours as hard as you can imagine. Most of the homes had tin roofs, and when the rain came the noise would be so loud that you could not hear anyone speaking. Then the sun would come out, and you felt as though you were in a steam bath for the rest of the day and into the evening.

MAY 29, 1960

I am all settled in Mazatenango now and working hard trying to get some more people baptized. We have a branch of 69 here and have quite a problem with inactive members. For example, tonight in sacrament meeting we had an attendance of 49 people, and a lot of those were investigators. We are trying to work out a plan with the members so that more people come out to meetings. Also I am organizing a choir so that we can tour the district of Mazatenango singing in all of the branches. We have a good Relief Society and Primary and a very good branch in general. I have two counselors in the branch presidency, and I am sure that in very little time one of them could be branch president, leaving me free to do more missionary work. I love to work in the branches because it really gives you a chance to develop many talents. Today I had to teach the member class and I gave them a lesson about revelation. It really was good and we are all trying to live so close to the Lord that each minute we can receive His inspiration and revelation when we need it.

My new companion was named Donald Cloud. He had some Indian blood in him and had grown up as a boy on the Church cattle ranch in Florida. He had spent most of his life before his mission on the back of a horse and had even roped in rodeos in Florida. He was a real cowboy. He was a wonderful companion. He was very quiet and worked hard. He talked with a little southern accent, even in Spanish. I always hated to lose a companion, but the new one would be just as wonderful most of the time.

*Mazatenango District Missionaries.*

In Mazatenango we lived with a member family by the name of Garcia. The father was a music teacher in the local school and was quite an educated man. There were several well-educated members in Mazatenango. One of the counselors in the branch presidency was a man by the name of Pedro Fernandes, who worked for a large book company selling books to schools. He seemed to read all the books he sold, which gave him a good education.

I soon began visiting the elders in my district with my companion. One morning we arose at 2 AM to catch the train to Còaptepeque. It was quite a train. It ran on a narrow-gauge railroad and was an old-time steam engine. We arrived at 5 AM and spent the day visiting with and teaching the elders who worked there. They were good missionaries—Antonio Yu Way and David Martinez. Elder Yu Way was Chinese, married, and had four children. He was approximately thirty-five years old when I met him. He had a delightful spirit, very positive and upbeat. He spoke Chinese, read English, and of course his Spanish was as native as could be. His family owned a large store in Tegucigalpa, Honduras, where he had been baptized as a young man. It was unusual that someone married and his age would be called to serve a full-time mission. However, Elder Yu Way's desire was so strong and the family had the means to support him, so somehow he was called to serve as a missionary. At that early period in the history of missionary work in Central America, there were few native Central Americans who were prepared to serve as full-time missionaries. Elder Yu Way and the few others like him were a great asset to furthering the work in the mission. Elder Martinez was from Mesa, Arizona, and was a Mexican. He spoke English, which made him doubly valuable because of his native Spanish. In those days we had no systematic method of teaching the gospel. We simply had to develop our own lessons to teach the basic principles of the gospel. We spent considerable time with these two missionaries helping them to develop a more effective lesson about the Apostasy. I believe our visit helped them a great deal. We spent the night with them and returned by train to Mazatenango the next day.

> JUNE 5, 1960
>
> My testimony of the gospel grows and grows the more I work with these people down here. We help them so much, not us but that which we teach them. We can see the hand of the Lord in everything that we do, He puts words in our mouths, and He leads us to the pure in heart if we are humble and prayerful. His Spirit keeps us from discouragement and gives the power we need to preach repentance to this Lamanite people from dawn to dusk. I am in the work of the Lord, and I am in it with all my heart, mind, and strength, and I know that if I give Him any less than my best, I am unworthy to be called an elder. Elder—that is the best name in the whole world, better than president, Mr., sir, señor, or whatever it might be. I pray that I might magnify more and more this priesthood that I hold, that I might have even more power than I now have so I can be a better servant of the Lord.

> JUNE 12, 1960
>
> The other day we were out knocking on doors. We knocked on one, and the man came to the door and told us he didn't want whatever we were selling. I tried talking to him a little, but the more I talked, the madder he would get. About then a big bulldog rounded the corner of the house and headed straight for me. He didn't bark or say a word, and I could see that he had blood in his eyes, but before I could move he had a hold of my leg and was chewing on it. I was really scared, but finally I got loose and kicked him a few times, and he took off. He ripped my new suit pants and tore my sock up and left a few teeth marks in my leg. He didn't like me, and the feeling was mutual.

By this time in my mission, I had been hit in the back by a dirt clod, chased by innumerable dogs, bitten by a bulldog, and chewed out by young and old and plainly told where to go with my message. To me it has always been interesting that instead of discouraging me, these kinds of experiences only made my resolve to share the message of the Restoration much stronger. I suppose that persecution can affect us in one of two ways—it can discourage us or strengthen us. For me, anytime I received any kind of persecution, something inside of me would be set off, and I was filled with an unquenchable desire to redouble my efforts in preaching the gospel.

About this time I had the opportunity of visiting the elders in Retalhuleu, where I had served before going to Tecpan. My companion and I had a good time with these elders, and I was particularly pleased to see how the work had progressed in that city. There were many baptisms, and I felt that we must work harder in Mazatenango to keep up with the work in Retalhuleu.

On Sunday, June 12, 1960, I sang a duet in sacrament meeting in Mazatenango with Brother Arturo Garcia, the man with whom we lived. He had a nice voice and was a music teacher, and we always enjoyed singing together. On that occasion we sang "O Jesus, Mi Gran Amor." It was a hymn out of the Spanish hymnbook, which contained many hymns that we never sang in English. I think one of the things I enjoyed most during my mission was singing. Seldom did we ever have a discussion with people in their homes without first singing with them one of the hymns. Each morning as we held our companion study before leaving the house, we would always commence with a hymn and then have a prayer. I loved singing with my companions and with the other elders in district or mission meetings. There were times when people would not let us into their homes and we would sing to them from the street. These people loved music, and many doors were opened, hearts touched, and the Spirit felt very strongly by investigator and missionary alike as the gospel was taught after the singing and praying. I am sure it is probably just a touch of nostalgia in thinking back of visiting in the humble homes of those wonderful Lamanite people, but I still get warm all over as I recall sitting around a table with a humble little family, having only a single candle for light, singing "Abide with Me; 'Tis Eventide" with them and my companion. More often than not, the candle would be one that we had brought with us. Because of the poverty of the people, in many instances when it got dark they simply went to bed. In order to bring the light of the gospel into these homes, we also had to bring the physical light as well. Nothing can invite the Spirit into our lives and homes like the singing of sacred hymns.

My love for the hymns has blessed me throughout my life. One night in the intensive care unit of the trauma center where I was taken after my accident, I was experiencing for the first time feelings much like I suppose one would experience who had claustrophobia. I did not know how I could possibly make it through the night. A young high councilor was sitting at my bedside and sensed that all was not well with me—at that time I couldn't speak. He said, "President Rushton, would you like me to sing to you?" I blinked my eyes once, which was the way I communicated a "yes" answer. He took out his little hymnbook and started to sing to me in the most beautiful baritone voice imaginable the hymns that I loved. The Spirit descended upon me gradually, and without even realizing what had happened, I soon fell into a peaceful sleep. Experiences similar to that have been repeated a number of times during the years I have been paralyzed. There is truly a great power in the hymns of this Church, a power that I discovered as a young missionary.

> June 26, 1960
>
> Last week we went to Coatepeque, and I'll tell you all about it so you will know how the Lord watches over us. Coatepeque is about three or four hours away from Mazatenango. To get to it, one has to go to Retalhuleu and take an old dirt winding road. Sunday night at 7:30 PM we went to the park to wait for the bus, but we waited out in the rain until ten o'clock, and it never did come. Some men in a gas station told us that a bus left at 4:30 AM, so we went to bed and got up at 4 AM because we had to be in Coatepeque before 8 AM. The 4:30 AM bus never came, so at 6 o'clock we took a bus to Retalhuleu to see what we could find there. At about 7:30 AM we were on the outskirts of Retalhuleu, which is a good two hours from Coatepeque, wondering what to do because we just knew that we would never get to Coatepeque in time. About then a Jeep came by. I hollered at it, and it stopped. We asked the owner where he was going, and he told us to Coatepeque and for us to get in. He was a German and a rich ranch owner that lived near Coatepeque. He knew of a special road to Coatepeque. He put that Jeep on it, and at five minutes to eight we pulled into Coatepeque. We just couldn't believe it. It was like a miracle. And it was just one of the few things that happens every day.

During my mission I always seemed to miss sending my dad a Father's Day greeting. There was no official Father's Day in Latin America. There certainly was no need for one inasmuch as the men were the "chiefs" and always *numero uno* (number one), if not in their families' minds at least in their own. The women could have used a Mother's Day each month and truly were the glue that kept that society together.

The first Sunday in July of 1960 we had a district conference in Mazatenango. Steve Covington, second counselor in the mission presidency, conducted the leadership meeting on Saturday afternoon. Steve was quite a showman and a great motivator. He had spotlights, special music, and really got our priesthood leaders inspired and motivated. He also held a special meeting with the elders in our district and gave us a stirring call to repentance. He had several airline tickets in his hand (probably not real) and told us that we should avail ourselves of them to go home if we were not willing to put more effort into the work. He had the elders in my district shaking in their boots. There had not been a single baptism in Mazatenango for a year. President Hancock sent me there based on my success in Ahuachapan. I felt pretty good about Elder Covington's talk because the Lord had led us to some great people that would be baptized, if all went well, within a few weeks.

Steve Covington was an interesting character in the mission field and continued to be so throughout his life. He was a great teacher, leader, and motivator. Upon returning from his mission, he and I and several other returned missionaries from Central America lived together at BYU and taught at the old Language Training Mission that later became the MTC. Steve went on to become a great opera singer. He has a marvelous tenor voice and sang for years for the San Francisco Opera Company. He now lives in the Palm Springs area and has had me speak to the youth of his ward and has performed in a concert in our Orange California Stake.

JULY 3, 1960

> We had 236 people out to conference, which is the biggest crowd that has ever been to a district conference here in Mazatenango. There were 50 priesthood holders out to the conference. It was a beautiful sight seeing all of those Lamanite men assembled there in that room with the power of God. What a marvelous thing is the priesthood! I wish that every man in the Church knew what it really is and what power it can give to you. It makes weak men strong and strong men stronger. Anyway, those men had it. I got to speak to them, and it was an experience that I shall never forget.
>
> In a few days I will have but ten short months left in my mission, and then this phase of my life will be over. I almost dread the day I have to leave this mission because in the last days the Lord is pouring His Spirit out on this Lamanite people, and the curse they have been living under is being lifted. I love them; they are truly my brothers and sisters.

> Everything is fine. I'm well and strong, and I will baptize some of these people before I leave this town. The Lord helps us when we want to be helped and if we but work.

Although I have already referred to the following incident, I thought I would like to include it as I experienced it in the mission field.

> July 10, 1960
>
> Saturday I received a letter from the cook in Ahuachapan, and she told me that she had gotten baptized. She said, "Elder Rushton, I am grateful for all that you did for me and for being so good to me and for teaching me the gospel. I am writing to you to tell you that now I am your sister." I believe that was the best letter I have ever received—to think that this fine woman got baptized. She was almost ready when I left, and she did it. Elder Prina (my boyhood friend from Ely, Nevada) wrote me a letter (he is in El Salvador) and told me how she had prayed hard that the Lord would open her ears so she could hear the gospel, and later she went to church and heard every word that was said. Remember that she is so deaf we had to holler at her to tell her what kind of beans we wanted. The Lord is at work in Central America, and I can feel His help every day and have seen His hand in the missionary work.

Things were beginning to pick up in Mazatenango. We were getting sixty people out to Sunday School and having some great lessons. I loved teaching the gospel to these humble and receptive people. We were getting a number of people ready for baptism in the first part of August. We had tracted out a man by the name of Oliva on June 6, and he never missed a Sunday meeting from the first day we met him. We also had found a great family by the name of Ordonas, seven of whom were of baptism age. They also never missed a Sunday meeting from the first day we met them. We were working on getting them married, and the father was not yet quite convinced that Joseph Smith was a prophet, but I had complete faith that he would come to know the truth and that the family would be baptized in August.

My companion and I took another trip to Coatepeque to work with the elders. We had to send Elder Martinez to Guatemala City because he was very sick. While we didn't know the extent of his problem, sickness was a real problem with all of the missionaries in Central America and in Guatemala in particular. Up to that time in my mission, I had missed only two days of work because of sickness, which was unusual and a great blessing. While in Coatepeque, I had the opportunity of working with the choir and playing the piano for them. Neither of the elders could play the piano, and the people loved to have anyone there who could do so.

> JULY 17, 1960
>
> My music has really helped me throughout my mission, and I give thanks to my Father in Heaven that I learned how to play the piano. I love music, but I doubt very much if I make it my career like I had planned. In fact, I am positive I won't. Right now we don't eat very well, but it is clean, and that is what is important. I will never eat like I ate in Ahuachapan. Boy, that old sister could really cook—made good hotcakes too.

# CHAPTER 10

# *Chimaltenango*

Things can change rapidly in the mission field. I would not be in Mazatenango to baptize the good people we had prepared. The Lord and President Hancock had other plans for me. I was called to be the president of the Chimaltenango District. In a very minor sense, this was the equivalent of serving as a stake president. I would be responsible for supervising the work of the ten elders in the district and also watching over four branches, which consisted of about 250 members. The branches were in the towns of Chimaltenango, Patzicia, Patzun, and Tecpan. I was elated to be able to return to the mountains and work once again with the pure Mayan people.

August 1, 1960

Saturday I got to go back to Tecpan again, and it hasn't changed a bit. We had a nice visit with the elders, and I had to audit their books. That night I talked in sacrament meeting, and it was really nice to see all of the old Tecpan members. My companion, Elder Farrer, and I

> sang a duet in the meeting—"Jehova Mi Pastor Es." He is a really good piano player, and we get along real well. Tecpan is still a tough town to do missionary work in, but the elders there are doing a fine job. It is just beautiful here in this Lamanite district now with the pine trees and corn growing everywhere. Everything is just beautiful and green and cold. It is such a change from Mazatenango that I still have the shivers and have to use two or three blankets every night.
>
> Last week we went to visit the elders in Patzicia also. Patzicia is one of the littlest towns in the whole district or mission but has a membership of about 80 members. They are all little old poor Indians, and they just worship the elders. All my mission I have wanted to work in Patzicia, but I never made it. Now that I am president of the district, I get to work there quite a bit. Anyway, last week we went there to work with the elders and to study the gospel with them. There is a grove of pine trees just outside of Patzicia up on a little hill overlooking the valley, and from the grove one can see almost the whole country. About 10 in the morning, we walked up to the grove to pray and study the gospel for a little while before we started working again. I really felt the Spirit of the Lord in that grove when we all knelt down in the grass and prayed to Him to help us to do His work among His covenant people, the Lamanites. Then we sang "We Thank Thee, O God, for a Prophet." All of the elders (Joel Martinez, Wakefield, and Farrer) have very good voices, and it was a very inspiring meeting.

While still visiting in Patzicia, I interviewed three people for baptism. Seventeen people had been baptized in that little town that year, and the elders had high expectations for many more before the end of the year. Forty or more years later, I can still feel the love I had for these simple, humble Mayans. Although their Spanish was not good and the women spoke only the Indian dialect, they sensed that we had the priesthood and were servants of the Lord. Attending a sacrament meeting was an interesting experience. All of the women and children sat in front of the chapel, which was really just a large room. They all wove their own cloth in their little homes. The color and pattern of the cloth they used for their blouses had been handed down from generation to generation. Seeing them all sitting together with the little children and babies strapped to their backs or held in their arms was a very colorful experience. Sitting behind the women and children were the men and older boys. They were dressed in white pants, white shirts, and dark blue coats. They all went barefoot or wore sandals—oftentimes made out of discarded rubber tires.

All of the talks were given in Spanish but would be translated into the native Indian dialect, Cachiquel. The same pattern was followed in the teaching of families in their homes. We would teach the men, and they would then translate what we had said and teach the women. The women did not speak Spanish, but as we taught the men we could feel the faith and trust these women had in what we were saying. They were wonderful, sweet, Christlike people. For about a year after I returned from my mission, I found it so difficult to even tolerate most Americans with whom I associated. I missed, more than I could ever express, the absolute openness, love, lack of materialism, and humility manifested by my Lamanite brothers and sisters.

My companion, Elder Farrer, and I spent a great deal of time visiting with the ten elders and members living in the Chimaltenango district. I went many nights in a row without sleeping in a bed. For example, the elders in Patzicia lived behind a gas station just outside of town alongside the Pan-American Highway. Their room was a very small adobe hut that contained two beds, a table, and two chairs. The beds did not have springs, only wooden slats upon which a mattress filled with cornhusks was laid. They did not have electricity or any kind of heat in a very foggy, damp, and cold climate. When visiting with those elders, we just rolled up in a blanket on the floor and did the best we could, hoping the night would quickly speed by. While visiting in Tecpan or Patzun where the elders had better accommodations, we would rent mattresses similar to the corn husk ones described above. One night in Patzun I forgot to tuck my pajamas into my socks, and I also did not sprinkle the bed with flea powder. I had been lying down for just a few moments when I felt like I was being carried out of my bed by fleas. I screamed and jumped to my feet, trying to get the fleas off my legs. I counted seventeen flea bites on just my left leg from my ankle to the knee. It was really a terrifying experience. Flea bites would have fit in very well with the kinds of afflictions experienced by Job in the Old Testament. Once you were bit, your greatest desire was to scratch the bites, which itched abominably. The trouble was that if you scratched the bite, although you would get some temporary relief, a few minutes later the bite would itch worse than before. Many elders would scratch the flea bites by scraping a knife blade over them and then pouring alcohol on to the bleeding sore. To me the quickest and best way to get rid of the bites was to do nothing and just try to exercise self-control, which was extremely difficult to do. Such were some of the challenges of working in the Indian villages.

AUGUST 10, 1960

Yesterday we had a district meeting and "preparation day" in Chimaltenango. It was the first preparation day I had experienced since coming into the mission 21 months earlier. Outside of town is a beautiful body of water created by natural springs. This lake is surrounded by huge pine trees and meadows. When we got there we started playing football, and did we ever have fun! The south end of the district and the district president (me), stood the north end of the district. We tramped them 20 to 12 after a hard fought game of about two hours. Boy, were we ever stiff and sore! It was the first time I had been off a walk in about 21 months. After the game we sat down and ate about six sandwiches and a stalk of bananas a piece. We were really happy and enjoying ourselves greatly. After the meeting we walked up a little hill and sat down among the towering pines and sang a hymn. Afterward we all knelt down in the grass and prayed. It seemed as though the Lord was right there with us. As the elders bore their testimonies out there on the hillside in that beautiful place, I was never so happy in my whole life. After they had all borne their testimonies, I stood up and gave them mine plus some instructions. It was the best missionary meeting that I have ever attended.

AUGUST 14, 1960

Tonight is Sunday, and I have been in Patzicia all day. We had a great day, and in the afternoon 90 people came out to sacrament meeting. It is really a blessing that I have to travel around to the different towns and visit the elders and members. I love Patzicia. I have always wanted to work here, and now I at least get to do so a little bit. All of the meetings are in Cachiquel except the talks of the elders, which are in Spanish.

Patzicia was opened to missionary labor about three years ago, and in that short time we have 89 members. They are all Indians, and the best people in the world. They tried to kill the first elders that worked here about two years ago, but through the good example of the elders the people now love us. The first man baptized was named Daniel Mich, who is a big leader among the people. He received a vision in which he saw the face of the prophet, David O. McKay. Because of his conversion, the whole Mich tribe are members of the Church. They love to sing, and each time I come we really go at it. They worship the elders, and we have got to be real careful because they are just like little kids and believe about anything that they hear. Everything we tell them they take as the gospel truth.

I must say that the conversion of Daniel Mich was a most significant event in the spreading of the gospel among the people in those little Indian villages. The elder who baptized Brother Mich was a young man by the name of Berkley Arnold Spencer. I have included his account of the beginning of missionary work in Patzicia and of the conversion of Daniel Mich in appendix A. It is an inspiring story, and I believe it deserves a first-person, eyewitness account. The history of the beginning of missionary work in Patzicia was taken from the writings and journal of Elder Spencer, junior companion to Nello Earl Deschamps, the first two missionaries in Patzicia.

Truly, Brother Mich had been chosen by the Lord and foreordained to accept the gospel in that little Indian village as taught to him by two humble elders. It was my privilege to get to know Brother Mich very well and to share a significant event in his life, as well as my own, which will be written about later.

AUGUST 14, 1960

I pray that I can stay well and healthy so that I can keep carrying this great gospel message to these Lamanites here so that many will gain their salvation.

I can see my patriarchal blessing being fulfilled right to the last letter. I have been called to preside over my brethren, and I pray that I can be humble and prayerful in the new calling that I have. If I am, I know that I will do a great work among my brethren and the Indians.

I hope that I never lose the vision of my mission and remember that I am here to baptize these good people and for no other reason.

AUGUST 24, 1960

I am sorry not to have written sooner, but I just haven't had time. It seems like I'm just running all of the time. This past week in just two days I interviewed 12 people for baptism, which is an awful lot of people. You can't imagine how the work is going along here in this district of Indians. My, how the Lord is blessing us with baptisms and converts! I feel like I have really been blessed being called to be the president of such a fine district. I pray that I can be humble and prayerful and diligent in my new calling. I have now been district president one month. The time just flies by so fast you wonder where it all goes. I have just 8 short months left in my mission. It seems like when you get to where you can really convert the people it is time to go home.

It wasn't all work, however. A short distance from Chimaltenango was the city of Antigua. The entire district of 12 elders walked from Chimaltenango to Antigua and back for our preparation day. It was probably a three to four mile walk each way but was well worth the effort.

There were more Catholic cathedrals, it seemed to me, in Antigua than there were houses, and the people were extremely fanatical. There were elders working in the city about two years before we walked into Antigua that morning, but they had been run out of town by citizens wielding machetes. I can still remember the desire I had to receive the assignment to open Antigua to missionary work once again. However, this day we played the part of tourists, taking pictures with the cathedrals as a backdrop. Just outside of the city was an extremely lofty and foreboding volcano called the volcano of water, or in Spanish *El Vulcan de Agua*. I believe it was in the late nineteenth century that the volcano exploded and much of Antigua was buried under water along with most of its inhabitants. I wish I knew more of the history, but to us as missionaries there was felt a melancholy spirit brooding over the city. We felt that much wickedness had occurred in that location. Toward evening as we left the city and walked toward Chimaltenango, the farther we got away from Antigua the better we felt. There was a great spirit of love and brotherhood among the elders in our district, and I was enjoying the happiest and most productive time of my mission.

SEPTEMBER 21, 1960

I'm sorry I haven't written, but it finally happened. After 20 months, I finally got sick. I've been in bed for a couple of days with the flu (I think—there aren't any doctors here). Anyway, I have had high fevers and chills and an upset stomach. I haven't eaten for three days, but I feel much better now because my fever broke yesterday and I really sweat.

The sisters in the Relief Society really baby me and worry about the other elders too. I couldn't begin to number the home remedies they've given me. They've got more than Dad. One of the sisters wanted to give me a big shot of something with a needle. I guess you know how that went over. Anyway, I feel fine now, a lot skinnier but still plenty tough. Saturday the 24th, we are baptizing a boy called Julio Massarriegas. He has been visited only three months, but in that time he has read the Book of Mormon, Doctrine and Covenants, Pearl of Great Price, *Teachings of the Prophet Joseph Smith*, *A Marvelous Work and a Wonder*, and *Articles of Faith* by Talmage. My, what a testimony he has!

> He has paid $20 tithing since we explained it to him. What a good young Mormon he will be! He is 24. The eighth of October we will baptize eight more if they are all ready. Pray with us so that they will be ready. All they lack is the paying of their tithing.

I didn't have the flu as it turned out, but the early stages of infectious hepatitis. My body was just worn out from the hard work and bad food and water. We simply could not find a decent place to eat in Chimaltenango, and we could not cook in the room we rented in the little hotel in town. For several weeks preceding my sickness, all we ate was bananas covered with Eagle Brand milk. We would buy a stalk of bananas when they were green and hang it in our room. As the bananas ripened, we would eat them with the Eagle Brand milk. Eagle Brand milk came in a can and was very thick and sweet. However, we must have needed more in our diet than just bananas and milk.

I felt exhausted all the time and had no desire to eat. I spent a day or two in bed and then forced myself to work. There was so much to do, and I just could not lie in bed doing nothing. I felt so responsible for the work and began questioning myself with regard to my commitment. Was I really sick, or was it just all in my mind? I tried a number of the remedies that the sisters brought, but nothing seemed to work.

One Sunday morning toward the end of September, my companion and I caught an early bus to Patzicia. We got there in time for priesthood meeting with the brethren. I taught the lesson that morning, and when I finished I had to lie down behind the pulpit. I was too weak to stand on my feet. Elder Farrer and I caught the earliest bus we could back to Chimaltenango. I remember trying to walk to where the bus stopped; I could barely put one foot in front of the other. I also was beginning to feel very nauseated.

CHAPTER 11

# *The Hospital*

GUATEMALA CITY, GUATEMALA: OCTOBER 4, 1960

I'm sorry that I have not written for so long, but this time I have a good excuse. I've been in the hospital and haven't been able to write. I'll tell you the whole story.

The last time I wrote (September 21) I told you that I had been sick but was feeling better. That very day I started getting worse. I had lost my appetite and hadn't eaten anything for about a week. There are no doctors in Chimaltenango, so I just kept putting off seeing the doctor because it meant a trip to the capital. Finally on the 26th, my birthday (thanks for the card and check), I woke up vomiting, so we caught the first bus for Guatemala City. I went to the mission office and they sent me over to see Dr. Herrera, about the best doctor in Central America. He checked me into the hospital, saying I had either typhoid or hepatitis. After further tests, it proved to be hepatitis (I still look like a Chinaman). The first day, the 26th, they fed me two quarts of stuff through the veins with a huge needle. Today is the fourth of October, and they have fed me nine times through the veins (a bottle a day). I have been here for over a week now, and the doctor said I may be here

> about three or four more weeks. Now, do not get excited, because I'm fine now and am eating like a horse. As you know, it takes time to get over hepatitis, and therefore I'm here in the hospital flat on my back. It's a beautiful hospital, and they really treat me well. The only thing I do not like is the bath they give me every day and going to the toilet in bed; otherwise it is fine.
>
> At first I was very disappointed and saddened, but I know that I've just got to have patience. I have a lot of it. I feel that it is a good experience because I had never ever before been in a hospital to stay. I have gained a lot of understanding and compassion for the sick that I never had before. I hope I never forget what it feels like to really be down and out.
>
> "I have had a chance to do a lot of reading being here and I just read a book that Dad would really like. It is called *Giant of the Lord.* It is the autobiography of a man called James S. Brown. He was in the Mormon Battalion, at Sutter's Fort in 1849, etc. really a great book.

The morning we left Chimaltenango I was so sick I thought I would die. When I got up that morning and looked in the mirror, I saw that I was yellow all over—even the whites of my eyes. We knew we had to get to Guatemala City to get some medical help. We went to the bus stop, and I began to throw up so violently that I broke my umbrella that I was leaning on in half. The bus that morning was filled with little Indians, their pigs, roosters and chickens, and assorted goods the Indians were taking to the market to sell. Fortunately, we were able to get into the front row of seats or I never would have made it to Guatemala City.

The smell from the unwashed Indians and their livestock was overpowering if you felt great, and if you were sick like I was, it was unbearable. I sat in that front seat hunched over with my face in my hands, trying to control the urge to throw up. It was the longest trip of my life, although Chimaltenango was only two or three hours away from Guatemala City.

The bus from Chimaltenango stopped at the large bus depot in Guatemala City, and we were able to immediately catch another bus to the mission home. My companion helped me off the bus and into the mission office. President Hancock came out of his office, and his first words were, "Elder Rushton, the statistics from your district for last week don't look very good." Without even a smile, I said, "President Hancock, I don't care!" With that statement he looked at me more closely and realized that I was very sick. However, he didn't know how really sick I was because instead of taking me to the hospital in the mission Buick, he had my companion take me out to the bus stop to catch a bus to the hospital. At any moment I thought I would just lose consciousness or something worse. We finally got to the hospital after another hour or so and walked into the lobby. The receptionist took one look at me and said, "You are sick, aren't you?" Immediately she took me from the waiting room into an adjacent room with a bed and had me lie down. In just a few minutes, Dr. Herrera, along with six or seven medical students, came walking into my room.

Dr. Herrera was one of the finest human beings I have ever met. He was the son of a wealthy father who had him educated in the United States and Europe. He attended MIT and a very prestigious medical school in Italy. His specialty was tropical diseases, and he was very knowledgeable about infectious hepatitis and how it should be treated. The hospital belonged to the family, and it was beautiful. I am sure that only the very rich of Guatemala would ever see the inside of the hospital. Many of those who were treated there were from Europe or the United States. I was in isolation because my kind of hepatitis was contagious. I had a large room with a picture window that permitted me to look out on to a jungle-type setting. Dr. Herrera was very kind and did everything in his power to keep me from being discouraged while insisting that I stay in bed for a lengthy period of time; it turned out to be forty-three days. Every morning he would walk into my room, throw open the drapes, and say, *"Muy buenos dias!"* (Good day).

I would ask him when I could leave the hospital, and he would always say *"Mañana"* (tomorrow). He knew that if he let me up and out of the hospital that I would begin to do missionary work again and that I would probably be right back in the hospital, even sicker than before. For the rest of my life, I will owe him a debt of gratitude for his wisdom, which was far greater than that of an eager missionary wanting to serve the Lord. Being in isolation with no TV or visitors, he took mercy on me and brought me a radio. There was a classical music station in Guatemala City, which I listened to for many hours each day. Every day at noon they had a special hour of concertos, which I dearly loved. I must admit that I also listened to the seventh game of the 1960 World Series between Pittsburgh and New York—in Spanish, of course. I remember that Bill Mazeroski hit a home run in the ninth inning to win the series over the Yankees.

Other missionaries had told me that any lengthy stay in the hospital would totally destroy both my spirituality and desire to do missionary work. I vowed that such would not be the case with me. President Hancock brought me books to read, one of which I have mentioned already. My greatest reading, however, was in the scriptures. During my stay in the hospital, I read the Book of Mormon, the New Testament, and most of the Old Testament. I also read *Jesus the Christ* by James E. Talmage, *Teachings of the Prophet Joseph Smith,* and *Essentials in Church History* by Joseph Fielding Smith. I was alone most of the time, with no distractions, and, after the first week, feeling quite well but awfully weak, I put myself on a strict schedule of reading. I would lie there in my bed, listening to classical music and devouring what I was reading. I was blessed with a great spirit of concentration and retention. It was probably the longest extended spiritual experience I have had in my life. When I was finally released from the hospital, although it was difficult to walk physically because I was in bed so long, spiritually I was walking in the clouds. I felt extremely close to the Lord and to the Prophet Joseph Smith. I had a fire burning within me to make the last six months of my mission the very best. My stay in the hospital turned out to be the necessary preparation for what would follow in Guatemala City.

The following are some random reflections regarding my forty-three days in the hospital in Guatemala City. I learned something about nurses. There were those who, when it was time to give me my bed bath, would bring in lukewarm water and barely do the job because they were so squeamish. Then there were those who came in with wonderful hot water and scrubbed me down and rubbed my back with lotion, which felt incredibly good to someone who was spending so much time in bed. When I could finally have visitors, President Hancock wouldn't let anyone come and visit because he wanted them out doing missionary work. However, Elder Myron Rigby would come to visit me once each week. We didn't talk about it, but I think the president gave him permission to come and make these visits. Oh, how I enjoyed talking to a fellow missionary! He was a gregarious and happy person and would make me feel so good.

When I had approximately two weeks left in the hospital, a young man from Switzerland was placed in a bed in my room. He had been in the hospital several weeks before I arrived and was more sick than I had been. He had come to visit his uncle and aunt who owned a large coffee plantation in Guatemala. When he disembarked from the ship, the government officials gave him several shots and apparently did so with a dirty needle. He contracted hepatitis and spent his entire vacation in the hospital trying to recover. As he began to feel a little better, we visited with each other. He spoke German, a little English, and a smattering of Spanish. I spoke English and Spanish, and somehow we were able to communicate quite effectively with one another. He told me much about his life in Switzerland, being in the army, working in a factory, and many other experiences. I asked President Hancock if he could locate a German Book of Mormon. He did so, and this young man consumed it. He was so excited about the book that when his aunt and uncle came to visit him that's all he would talk about. As I recall, they were less enthusiastic about it than he was. I was released from the hospital before he was, and it was an emotional farewell. We had become good friends in that short period of time. I lost track of him, and to this day I do not know whether he was ever baptized. I hope that he found the missionaries when he returned to Switzerland. Dr. Herrera told me as I was leaving that the best thing that had ever happened to the young man from Switzerland was to spend two weeks with me in that room. I consider it a compliment to the Church, the gospel, and young missionaries in general.

OCTOBER 21, 1960

I feel real swell. I'm as weak as a kitten, haven't had a haircut for five or six weeks, and I really am a tough looker. The nurse shaved me today because she said I look like Fidel Castro. Now I look like Davy Crockett.

I've been receiving a lot of letters lately, and everybody seems quite concerned. I guess everyone is more worried than I am. I guess it's a pretty dangerous disease, and you have to be careful.

Since I've been here, I've read the Book of Mormon, the New Testament, and most of the Old. I've now read the Book of Mormon five times altogether (twice in Spanish). It's the best book that has ever been written. I'm reading *Jesus the Christ* for the third time now, and someday I'll have a fairly good knowledge of the gospel.

OCTOBER 28, 1960

Well, I'm still in the hospital, but I feel real well. They will take new blood tests the second of November, and they will be able to tell me for sure when I can leave the hospital.

Today the barber came and gave my partner and me a haircut. He had a pair of electric clippers, and it was one of the few times in my mission that I've had my hair cut with electric clippers. I look pretty sharp now because we got to shave today also.

I just finished reading *Jesus the Christ*, and it's the best book that I've ever read with the exception of the Book of Mormon.

I hope that you are getting my letters now because I know that you are worried because I am in the hospital. The doctor says I'm getting better, although slowly, and I'm sure I'll be fine in a little while.

NOVEMBER 7, 1960

Tomorrow is my last day in the hospital. I have been here a long time, and I'm really happy to be going. President Hancock came to see me on Friday and said that he wasn't going to send me back up to Chimaltenango. He told me that I have just worked myself down to the point I didn't have any resistance to sicknesses. Then when I got sick I didn't come down but stayed and thought I would get better. He said, "I won't send you back up to kill yourself." He said that he was going to make me supervising elder of one of the two districts here in Guatemala City if I get in good enough shape to handle it. It's a lot of responsibility, and I pray that I get well enough to do it. I'm sure that I will. The doctor has told me that for the first two weeks he doesn't want me to work—just lie around. I don't know if I'll be able to "lie around"; that's the toughest job I've ever had. I hope and pray that after these two weeks I'll be in top shape. I have to see the doctor at the end of the two weeks, and then I'll know how I am. The president won't give me the job until I am in good shape. I have always wanted to work in Guatemala City and I'm sure that the Lord wants me to work here also.

At the time, I did not realize that I was being prepared for the six-month hospital stay I would endure after my accident in the ocean in 1989. It never ceases to amaze me how so many of my missionary experiences helped to prepare me for what would follow in my life. It has caused me to have a firm testimony that indeed the Lord is all-knowing.

# CHAPTER 12

# *Guatemala City*

November 15, 1960

It is now November 15, and I am out of the hospital and am feeling very well. I am the supervising elder in Guatemala City, region 2 of the city. I have to supervise about 20 elders and sisters, which is really a lot of work, and that is why I haven't written to you sooner. I imagine that within about a week I'll be all straightened out. I go to the doctor Friday, and he'll tell me if I'm well or not yet. I feel good, but I get tired really fast. I pray that I can gain my full strength again. This is my new address: 3 Avenida 1342 Zona 1 Guatemala City, Guatemala. All is well!

The time when I was released from the hospital is still indelibly engraved in my memory. President Hancock called me to be the supervising elder before I left the hospital, and he assigned me two junior companions. When I left the hospital, I could barely walk, and my feet felt like two big flat tortillas. My leg muscles had atrophied, and I had no calluses on my feet. I literally could only just hobble along by clinging to one of my companions. These two green missionaries had recently arrived from the United States and were anxious to get out and begin doing some missionary work. One of these elders, Elder Lynn Jensen from southern California, would remain a lifetime friend. Elder Myron Rigby and his companion had just moved out of a beautiful home in Guatemala City, and we moved in to their vacated room. Elder Rigby was the elder who visited me while I was in the hospital. This was by far the best lodging I had ever experienced during my entire mission.

I can't remember how we got from the hospital to our new home, but it was probably by public transportation. The next morning we got up, and my two new companions, who didn't speak a word of Spanish, wanted to go out and start preaching the gospel. They realized that I couldn't go, but I told them how to catch the bus and where to get off—in zone 12. I thought they would be okay and hoped they would return safely. I lay in my bed reading and wishing I was with them. They had only been gone what seemed like a short time when they came rushing into our room as excited as any two missionaries could be. They told me they got off the bus where I had told them to and knocked on the door of the first house they came to. A friendly, smiling woman opened the door and laughed out loud at their attempts to communicate. However, by pointing at the Bible and the Book of Mormon they had in their hands, she got the idea that they wanted to teach her and her family about Jesus.

What you need to know is that Lynn Jensen was the most gregarious, outgoing, and uninhibited person that I had ever met. He was about six feet three inches tall and must have looked like a giant to those small Guatemalan people. He was an extremely fun-loving and happy spirit. He had instant rapport with the people despite the fact he couldn't speak any Spanish. Once inside the home, these new and very green missionaries pulled out their little hymn books and began singing to the children and mom and dad as well as they could. Elder Jensen had a good voice and loved to sing. As he and I worked together when my strength began to return, we did a lot of singing in the streets and homes of the wonderful people in Guatemala City. As we knocked on doors, if we were not permitted to enter we would oftentimes sing out in the street, especially songs that the little children loved. This served to both endear us to the people and open many hearts and doors. Anyway, this little family was so impressed with these two young men from the United States who had such an obvious wonderful spirit about them that they insisted they come back the next day with somebody who could speak Spanish.

I tried to calm them down, but they were like a couple of kids on Christmas Eve as they eagerly anticipated returning to the home of that family. Early the next morning they carried and dragged me out to the bus stop, and we rode through the streets of Guatemala City to the home of this family. I can remember how weak and lightheaded I was from this exertion. However, there was never any question as to whether I would go, and this was the end of my recuperation period. There were just too many people to teach and too many missionaries to work with for me to lie around the house. As we got off the bus, we could see this radiant woman waiting for us standing in the doorway of her humble home. Her husband was a shoemaker, and they had four little children. What a welcome we received! We sang some more, and then I taught them. The preparation I did in the hospital was evident as I taught this family under the influence of the Spirit more powerfully than I had ever taught during my mission. This would be one of the most wonderful conversions I would witness during my mission, and I will return to the details later in the story.

It was about this time that President Hancock arranged for Elder Jensen and me to drive with him and Sister Hancock in the mission Buick up to Patzicia. The branch had grown so much that President Hancock felt impressed that it was time to call a native Mayan Indian to be the branch president. He didn't tell me at the time why he was taking me with him, but as the day unfolded and he issued the call to Daniel Mich to be the branch president, President Hancock indicated that he wanted me to set Brother Mich apart. Brother Mich's conversion was truly miraculous, and he surely was foreordained to be a pivotal figure in bringing the blessings of the gospel to the people of his village and the surrounding area. By having me set Daniel Mich apart as the president of the Patzicia Branch, I believe that President Hancock was rewarding me for the work I had done in the Chimaltenango District. What a joy it was to me then and continues to be as I realize that I had the privilege of setting apart the first full-blooded Mayan in Central America as a branch president. This was a watershed event in the building of the kingdom of God among the Mayans of Guatemala.

NOVEMBER 21, 1960

I went to the doctor again, and he told me that I was much better, but he wanted to take more tests the third of December. I will be able to tell you then how I am. I feel much stronger each day and I am sure that I will soon be completely well.

All my mission I have prayed for a chance to work in Guatemala City because this is the place where more baptisms come from. With the Lord's help, I will see a lot of baptisms down here.

There is a man that lives in the next room by the name of Jorge Caim. He is from Lebanon and recently was baptized and is one of the greatest men I have ever known. He has made and lost millions of dollars in Mexico City, from which he recently came. He still is worth

> many thousands, and within a month he will open a restaurant in the new Hilton Hotel of Guatemala City, which will be the highest building here. I bet that he will be the first stake president of a Latin stake in Zion. The minute he heard the gospel, he knew that it was true and he got baptized. I really enjoy talking to him because I have never known anyone as smart or a greater gentleman. He speaks English, Spanish, Arabic, French, and some others I don't know. I hope that you can meet him one day.

I was wrong about Brother Caim becoming the first stake president in Latin America, but he was the first bishop of the Church in Mexico City. My companions and I lived in the same home with him until I left the mission field six months later. He was wonderful in every way. He and his family had made a great deal of money in the textile business in Mexico. He had had a problem with the Mexican government that he never explained to me, except to say that if he had not left Mexico he would have been thrown in jail and possibly killed. Knowing him as I did, I don't believe that he was doing anything illegal, but in Mexico at the time there was no due process, so he had to literally flee for his life. The restaurant he was building in the new Hilton Hotel was beautiful, which was evidence that he and his family still had significant resources.

He came in contact with the Church while living in a pension (boardinghouse) in Guatemala City where Elder Myron Rigby and his companion were living. Their rooms were next to each other, and as they became acquainted with Brother Caim and he knew who they were, he had a desire to visit with them. He was interested in religion and had studied many of the religions of the world and so was eager to have the missionary discussions. I believe it was in the second discussion that as Elder Rigby bore his testimony that he had the priesthood authority to baptize and perform other priesthood ordinances, he was transfigured before Brother Caim. Brother Caim said that Elder Rigby had a light radiating from him that was supernatural, and Elder Rigby said of the experience that although he did not know what was happening, he never felt a more beautiful, warm, and comfortable feeling than on that occasion. Elder Rigby was a

*Elder Rushton and Jorge Caim.*

delightful person who emanated a spirit of enthusiasm for the work and love for the people. He and Brother Caim became extremely close friends. However impressive as this experience was to Brother Caim, it was not the ultimate factor in his conversion, but it was going to church the following Sunday and feeling the love and warmth of the members of the ward that made him know that this indeed was the Church of Jesus Christ.

Brother Caim was very much into living a healthy lifestyle. Each morning he would go to the roof on our home, which was flat, and spend an hour or so doing yoga. Being from Ruth, Nevada, I had never been exposed to the world of yoga. He was a vegetarian, although he would eat an occasional piece of meat and believed in using nature's products as opposed to those manufactured by man. Instead of using aftershave lotion, he would cut a lemon in half and squeeze the juice onto his face and then onto his hair before combing it. He was a distinguished and handsome gentleman and physically fit. Brother Caim was extremely formal in all that he did. How he put up with us I will never fully understand. Each morning we would invite him to study the scriptures with us and have prayer. Before we would begin our scripture study, we would always sing a hymn. Brother Caim was extremely tone-deaf, and either Elder Jensen or I would give the pitch, which we would all then hum together before beginning our singing. Brother Caim would always be at least a half pitch off the true note. It sounded so awful that Elder Jensen and I would get the giggles no matter how hard we tried to stifle them. We would roll on the floor, and Brother Caim would get offended, thinking we were making fun of him, which we really were not; we just could not control our laughter. He would walk out of the room, and we would have to go get him and tell him how much we loved him and that we were not making fun of him and would he please forgive us. Great man that he was, he would always come back and study with us and forgive us. Fortunately, we did not drive out the first bishop of Mexico City from the Church at this early stage of his membership.

NOVEMBER 28, 1960

I have just passed a glorious week of work here in the city of Guatemala. You can't imagine how the Spirit of the Lord is working among the Lamanite people and among the elders.

We tracted out a family of about six who can be baptized any day. We tracted them out on Friday, and this Saturday they would have been baptized if the mother hadn't caught a cold. We will baptize them this

> coming Saturday anyway. It is amazing to see how rapidly these people can gain great testimonies of the gospel. Elder Jensen and I have just been singing and bearing our testimonies to everyone we can and are seeing great success. Tonight we had one of our investigators get baptized. She is the most wonderful woman you can imagine. She and her husband weren't married, but last night we went with them to the courthouse and served as witnesses while she and her man got married. Tonight when she came out of the waters of baptism, her face was just glowing, and after we had confirmed her I thought that she would cry. We have visited her just two weeks. Can you imagine that? My, what a wonderful change comes into these people's lives when they accept the gospel.

This was the woman that my two junior companions contacted on my first morning out of the hospital. Later her husband would also be baptized. In 1994 as my son John served his mission in Guatemala City, he and his new companion went to visit some of the members of their new ward. His companion, who had already spent some time in the ward, said, "Let's go visit with the Relief Society president and her husband, the ward mission leader." As they walked up to the home, there was a woman out in front. John extended his hand and said, "Hello, I am Elder Rushton." The woman gave a little scream and ran into the house, returning within just seconds with a small photograph. She asked John if he knew who was in the photograph, and upon looking at it John said, "That's my dad when he was a missionary!" This woman, in 1960, during the month of December, led Elder Jensen and me to twenty-two relatives and friends who were baptized that month. In 1994, soon after my son John had met this family, the daughter, who was just a little girl with a physical handicap at the time of her parents' baptism, wrote me a letter that was soon followed by one from her younger brother who was then serving as a bishop in Guatemala City. Soon after these letters arrived in our home, they were somehow misplaced, and it was only recently that my wife found them in a file where they had been placed almost ten years ago. These two letters are found in the appendix.

Below is a letter that this wonderful woman, Gloria de Alvarado, wrote to me forty-three years after her baptism. She did not have my address, so she sent the letter by way of a missionary from Provo who had been serving in Guatemala. I have no idea what motivated her to send this letter after all these years. Was it because I was thinking of her as I wrote about this part of my mission? Her letter helped me to make things historically accurate in this part of the book.

Ciudad Real, July 18, 2003

Elder Rushton, I am Sister Alvarado of Guatemala and I am happy to greet you and tell you of the many blessings of our Heavenly Father to our family. You should have us in your journal. My husband and I lived in Petapa Avenue, Zone 12, when you and your companion in the mission visited us and gave us the discussions. I was baptized on November 26, 1960. You and your companion, Elder Jensen, took us to the municipal building in Guatemala City so we could be married. Since then my life changed, and I am happy to be a member of The Church of Jesus Christ of Latter-day Saints. My husband and I were sealed in the Arizona Temple in 1979. I have eight children—five returned missionaries and now two grandsons, one who is a missionary in San Salvador and one who returned from his mission in France. He and his parents live in Utah in the United States. Seven of my children are married, and all are members of the Church—two are bishops, and a daughter married a returned missionary from the United States, and they live in the state of Washington. All of us work in the Church. I tell you this so that you can feel happy to have served a mission in the city of Guatemala, and I thank you for the favor you did for me. Elder Rushton, I am very grateful to my Heavenly Father to have come to know the Church and this gospel of truth. Now I am working in the Guatemala Temple every Tuesday and Friday, and I am happy for this and am grateful to God for having permitted me to have this calling to work for Him.

Well, Elder Rushton if you could write to us my address is as follows . . . It would give us much joy to hear from you soon.

There is no way that I can begin to express how I felt when I received this information about the Alvarado family. I know in my heart that if she and her husband had been my only baptisms during my two-and-a-half-year mission, it would have been well worth all of the effort I expended and then some. Since receiving this letter from Sister Alvarado, I have been in constant contact through email with her son Eduardo, who was only two years old when we baptized his parents. He has served a full-time mission among the native Indian people in the mountains of Guatemala, where he learned their dialect. He is now serving for the second time as a bishop, has a beautiful family, and is a wonderful Latter-day Saint.

Guatemala City, November 28, 1960

Yesterday we had a meeting for all of the district presidents and supervising elders of Guatemala and received from the mission a new challenge to baptize in the month of December 700 people. Can you

> imagine that? We are going to need help. I've got to inspire my 20 elders to do it, and I know it is possible. You wanted to know what I wanted for Christmas. I'll tell you. I want to see 700 people baptized before New Year's Day, and that's all I want. Also, I want you to fast and pray for Central America, her people and missionaries. Pray that we baptize these 700 people. I'm going to write a letter to President Clair Black and all of the bishops back home to get everybody to have a special day of prayer and fast for us down here so that we will be able to fulfill the challenge that has been given to us by our inspired President Hancock.

I was not the only missionary in Central America who took this challenge very seriously. Today, of course, we would be forbidden to write and ask our stakes to fast and pray for the work in our mission, but then it was acceptable. In order to understand the enormous challenge we had been given, there were a little over three hundred convert baptisms in all of Central America in 1959. Our motto from the day we received this challenge from President Hancock was "Fast and Pray and Lead the Way." All of the missionaries wrote to their stake presidents as I had done—a date was chosen for the special day of fasting and prayer—and we were joined by all of our stakes in the United States. During most of my mission we fasted every Thursday because that was the day that we interviewed people for baptism. We planned to have a baptismal service every Saturday for those who were interviewed that previous Thursday. Today President Hancock might be criticized for setting a goal like this, but he felt that something must be done to kick us out of our comfort zone and move the work in Central America to a higher plateau. I will always believe that what happened in December of 1960 was the first rumblings of a gigantic eruption of baptisms and Church growth in the land of the Lamanites.

> DECEMBER 11, 1960
>
> This past week has really been a memorable one for me. Last night there were 21 people baptized in the city. Seven of them were investigators of Elder Jensen and me. Elder Jensen was a little sick, so I baptized all seven of them. Since November 15, Elder Jensen and I have baptized nine people into the Church. The Lord is really helping and blessing us, leading us to the honest and sincere people here in the city. In two weeks there have been 36 baptisms in Guatemala City, but we will need your prayers in our behalf if we hope to fulfill the huge challenge that we have of 700 people throughout the mission. Yesterday we had a special fast day, and I know that we will really be blessed in our great work.

I am feeling very well now, and each day I get stronger and feel like my old self. I really enjoy working with the elders, and I learn a lot from them. I hope that they learn a lot from me.

I would give anything if you could see how the gospel changes these people's lives. It makes them happy and really gives them something to live for. We baptized some of the most humble and sincere people I have ever seen Saturday night. A little girl called Maria was baptized, and on the way to the pila she wouldn't let go of my hand, and you could just feel the love and confidence that she had in me, believing me to be a servant of the Lord. It is humbling, and it is wonderful. If you ever want to feel real joy and a complete peace that just fills you until you want to burst, just preach repentance to a person, lead him to the baptismal font, and then watch and see the love and gratitude in his eyes as he leaves the water after having covenanted with the Lord to always obey His commandments. It is something you just can't explain; you have to do it to know it.

The longer that I am a missionary, the more I love the missionary work. It is the greatest work that anyone could ever do.

JANUARY 2, 1961

I was really thrilled when I received that telegram from President Black telling me that the Nevada Stake was going to fast. I thank you all for the fasting and I want to tell you the results of the month of December

*Elder Rushton and recently baptized family in Guatemala City.*

and for the year. To my knowledge, and it is an approximation, for the year 1960, there were 1,036 people baptized in the mission, more than 300 of them coming the last month of the year. In Region 2 of Guatemala, we had 39 baptized. My companion and I were privileged to bring many new people into the Church the month of December. Your prayers were answered in our behalf. I just can't tell you how much I appreciate it and love you for having prayed and fasted for us.

Although we did not achieve our goal of seven hundred baptisms in December, what we did achieve was phenomenal. In 1959 we had only a little over three hundred baptisms throughout the mission, and to go from that number of baptisms to over a thousand was remarkable. I truly believe to this day that our success was predicated upon fasting and prayer. We were the same missionaries working in the same villages and cities, but a new spirit began to cover Central America. We started teaching with faith and with the Spirit, and the Lord did the rest. From that year forward, there would never be fewer baptisms in Central America than in 1960. Of course, during the ensuing years as new missions have been formed, there have been thousands of baptisms in Central America each year.

JANUARY 2, 1961

This Christmas was the most wonderful experience of my life. Joseph Fielding Smith is touring South America with his wife and President Tuttle. They will be here on the seventh of January. However, President Tuttle came on up to Guatemala the 23rd of December and was here for Christmas. The first time I met him was at the baptismal service on Friday night. He asked me my name and when I told him, he asked me if I was related to Don Rushton. I told him that Don was my uncle, but he was dead now. He told me that Don was his first missionary companion in the Northern States Mission.

I really enjoyed talking to him. He is a great man. He said that Don could really make great hotcakes. For me it was very interesting because Don is the only uncle I didn't know. President Tuttle was also a marine on Iwo Jima. He served 18 months in the Pacific campaign.

On Christmas Eve I sang in a quartet, and President Tuttle, when he spoke to us, said that Uncle Don used to sing in a quartet also. I hope you get to meet him someday. You'll really like him.

My Uncle Don, one of my dad's younger brothers in a family of seventeen children, was a very wonderful and special person. I never met him personally. Of those seventeen children, he was the only one who was able to serve a full-time mission as a young man. He was not killed in combat during the war but rather suffered death as a result of an accident here in the United States as he was driving a tractor and working on one of the military bases.

President A. Theodore Tuttle, a member of the First Council of the Seventy, had been assigned to live in Montevideo, Uruguay, to oversee the missionary work in Latin America. This was a precursor to Area Presidents and the Quorums of the Seventy. I have very seldom ever met a more sensitive man than Elder Tuttle. He had very strong feelings about the ignorance and poverty of the nations of Latin America, which had been dominated by the Catholic Church for so many centuries. Whenever he would talk about the people and how they had been kept in ignorance, suffering so much because of it, he would become very emotional and could not keep back the tears.

Joseph Fielding Smith and his wife, Jesse Evans Smith, finally arrived and presided over a countrywide conference. As part of this experience, Joseph Fielding Smith interviewed each missionary individually. For some reason I cannot recall the interview I had with Elder Smith. I can remember that he appeared to be very austere and devoid of humor, which I feel now was a false perception as I have read and studied his life. His wife, however, more than made up for it. Jesse Evans Smith was Joseph Fielding Smith's third wife. His first and second wives both passed away (he was not a polygamist), and he married Jesse much later in life. Jesse was a noted vocalist and had been a soloist for the Tabernacle Choir for many years. Her brother was Richard L. Evans of the Quorum of the Twelve Apostles, who also wrote and read the spoken word each Sunday for the Tabernacle Choir broadcasts. She had never married, and her marriage to Joseph Fielding Smith was a great blessing to both of them. She was gregarious, outgoing, and full of fun. The Lamanite people in Guatemala loved her because of her great outgoing spirit. She was a wonderful companion to Joseph Fielding Smith as he traveled through Central America meeting with the missionaries and the Saints.

As President Smith interviewed the missionaries one-on-one, Sister Smith and Elder Tuttle entertained those who were not being interviewed at the time in the chapel by the mission home. She and Elder Tuttle both sang, and then each missionary or group of missionaries had to do something as part of the entertainment. When all of the missionaries had been interviewed, Joseph Fielding Smith rejoined the group, and Jesse insisted that he do something as part of the entertainment. He grumbled and didn't want to do anything, but Jesse kept pushing him, and it was fun for all of us to see this interaction between these two great people. Finally she said to him, "Joseph, tell that funny missionary story when you were a missionary in England." Well, he told the story, and for the life of us we could not see the humor in it. That, of course, made the entire experience that much funnier.

After the program, Joseph Fielding Smith instructed us about our missionary labors. I was sitting on the front row, and it seemed to me that he directed all of his remarks in my direction. He read to us Doctrine and Covenants 4, and every time he said the word *ye*—for example, "O *ye* that embark in the service of God, see that *ye* serve him with all your heart, might, mind and strength, that *ye* may stand blameless before Him at the last day"—he would point his finger at me, look me in the eyes, and emphasize the word *ye*. By the time he got through the entire section, I was perspiring heavily. For the rest of my life and even now whenever I read section 4, I have the vision in my mind of Joseph Fielding Smith looking me in the eyes, pointing his finger at me, and making this revelation intensely personal.

After having given us an hour or so of instruction, he opened up the lesson to questions and answers. For years Joseph Fielding Smith had a feature in the *Improvement Era* entitled "Answers to Gospel Questions." As young missionaries, here we had standing before us a living "Answers to Gospel Questions." This was like throwing red meat to a group of starving lions. A young elder sitting next to me shot his hand up, was recognized, and said, "Elder Smith, when will the Second Coming take place?" Elder Smith smiled and said, "That's an easy question to answer. He will come tomorrow!" All our mouths flopped open at that statement, and then he told us to turn to D&C 64. He read to us the following: "Behold, now it is called today until the coming of the Son of Man, and verily it is a day of sacrifice, and a day for the tithing of my people; for he that is tithed shall not be burned at his coming. For after today cometh the burning—this is speaking after the manner of the Lord—for verily I say, tomorrow all the proud and they that do wickedly shall be as stubble; and I will burn them up, for I am the Lord of Hosts; and I will not spare any that remain in Babylon" (D&C 64:23–24).

*Jessie Evans Smith and two Lamanite sisters from Coban.*

We got the point. Almost immediately an elder in the back of the chapel leaped to his feet and said, "Elder Smith, where are the lost ten tribes?" As I remember, the meeting came to a hasty conclusion, and, looking back, I think Joseph Fielding Smith was having a really good time with us. Our maturity level was not extremely high and was about on a par with our intelligence. What a joy it was to be able to meet and associate with this apostle of the Lord, his wife, and Elder Tuttle.

JANUARY 10, 1961

We just have finished the visit of the Smiths and Tuttles. Sunday we had 1,900 people out to conference, and it was really wonderful. I saw all of the people from the Chimaltenango District and Mazatenango and Quezaltenango. It was really a joy seeing all of those Lamanite people gathered together in one place. In the morning we had priesthood meeting, and there were at least 300 priesthood holders present. What a great power the Church is beginning to be down here among this people.

I am a little sad today because they took my companion, Elder Jensen, and sent him to Quezaltenango. I really love him, and right now I feel empty. But it will pass, and soon I will have a new companion.

Elder Jensen really deserves some additional comments. I was only with him for a short period of time, but in that time together we were guided to many choice people who we were able to baptize. It was, undoubtedly, the most productive part of my mission regarding convert baptisms. I was Elder Jensen's first senior companion, and he was delightful and exciting to work with. He was extremely outgoing and totally uninhibited in trying to speak Spanish and sharing the gospel with

*Jessie Evans Smith and Lamanites, Guatemala country conference.*

others. He had a very good singing voice, and we always sang together each morning as part of our study. We then sang in the homes of those we taught.

Elder Jensen and I would be walking down one of the streets in Guatemala City, and all of a sudden I would realize that he wasn't by my side. He would be in a shop bartering with the owner over some typical Guatemalan cloth or a new tie. I had to keep my eye on him to make sure he didn't wander off somewhere. Several times each month we would ride a train out to the little town of Amatitlan, outside of Guatemala City, to visit the members there and also to do some missionary work. On the way home at night we would ride on the very back of the caboose, and as we would pass groups of people Elder Jensen would wave at them and then light firecrackers and throw them off the back of the train. It was dark, and we went by so fast that I'm sure we were never identified. That was Elder Jensen for you. Did I ever throw any of the firecrackers? What do you think? Anyway, he was a great spirit, and together the Lord blessed us to do a great work.

I must also mention one of the sister missionaries I supervised in Guatemala City at this time. Her name was Alma Gloria Chavez. She was tall and slender and on fire with the message of the restored gospel. All the time I was in Guatemala City, she had the highest number of new converts in our district. She was an incredible missionary. She was from San Pedro Sula in Honduras, where she and her mother had been converted several years before I met her. She was a great Catholic theologian as a young student in Honduras. Each year there would be a countrywide test given on Catholic doctrine and practice, and her senior year in high school she received the highest score in all of Honduras. It was about this time that the missionaries found her and her mother and taught them the gospel. Alma and her mother were truly converted. When the local Catholic Church discovered that they were going to be baptized into the Mormon Church, every pressure was exerted against her and her mother to discourage them from taking this step in their lives. Alma even received a letter from Rome asking her to reconsider what she was doing and spelling out some of the consequences that would occur if she pursued her current course of action. This letter only strengthened their resolve, and they were baptized and became an important part of the branch in that city of Honduras. Not too long after their baptism, Alma accepted a mission call. Her mother had no way of supporting herself, so the members of the branch built a little hut on the church property where the chapel was, and she lived there until Alma finished her mission, receiving food and help from the members of the branch. With her knowledge of Catholic doctrine, you might imagine how she could teach the Catholic people in Guatemala City. With her command of the language and knowledge of the scriptures, she was probably the most powerful teacher I met while on my mission. I wonder what has become of Alma. I am sure that she has made a great contribution to the growth and strength of the Church in that part of Honduras. What a joy it was to work with her and feel the great spirit she possessed!

> JANUARY 31, 1961
>
> Last night we had a testimony meeting of our region, and it was the best I have ever been to. There have never been people I have loved any more than these elders and lady missionaries. I just pray that our associations and friendships will carry on even after our missions are through.
>
> The meeting lasted about three and a half hours, but we weren't aware of the passing of time. Almost everyone that spoke cried, including myself. I have done it only three times in my life: at my farewell, once two years ago in Quezaltenango, and last night in Guatemala City.
>
> I am glad I can feel the Spirit of the Lord to that extent because I just am not the crying kind, and it takes something powerful to bring the tears. All the elders and sisters expressed the love they had in their hearts for me and for the help I had given them, and hearing that just made me so happy I couldn't hold it in. I'll tell you about it someday.

*Elder Wadsworth, President Hinckley's nephew.*

There is a big difference between emotions and feeling the Spirit of the Lord. This and other testimony meetings with my fellow missionaries always seemed to bring the Spirit. The Spirit can make our feelings very tender and sensitive. When that happens, tears can flow regardless of our efforts to control them. I have discovered through the years that as I have become accustomed to feeling that special spirit that it takes quite an outpouring to bring the tears. I have read the accounts of some of the apostles who were present in the temple that day when President Kimball received the revelation that all men, regardless of their race, could have the full blessings and power of the priesthood in their lives. Tears were shed by these strong men, well acquainted with the Holy Ghost, who had never felt such an outpouring of the Spirit in their lives.

For some reason there is a scarcity of letters during this time of my mission in Guatemala City. I'm sure it was not my mother's fault for not saving them. More likely I was so busy and involved I wasn't writing as faithfully as I normally did. In writing this book about my mission, I painfully realize how important it is to keep a good journal. I can't remember the names of many people I baptized, or even the names of some missionary companions I had. The following is a re-creation, as best I can remember, of some experiences I had in Guatemala City.

After Elder Jensen was transferred to Quezaltenango, my new companion was Elder Wadsworth. Gordon B. Hinckley was his uncle (his mother was President Hinckley's sister). Elder Wadsworth had grown up near Panaca, Nevada, which is about 150 miles south of Ely. His father owned a large cattle ranch, and Elder Wadsworth had spent months at a time as a young boy out in the desert with the cattle. I was his first senior companion, and he was something. The first thing he told me when we met is that he liked cattle better than people. In the morning he would get up, put a cowboy hat on his head, stand in front of the mirror, and shave himself with a straight edge razor he would sharpen on a razor strap. He would then put on a pair of Levis, a Levi shirt, a big leather belt with a huge buckle on it, and then do his personal study and companion study in that attire. Just before we would leave the house for the day, he would change into his missionary suit, white shirt, tie, and missionary hat, which he always wore at a rakish angle on the back of his head. His Spanish was absolutely atrocious, but in spite of all of this he was a good companion and missionary. I enjoyed being with him, and because of his absolute honesty and sincerity he was like a breath of fresh air.

I should mention that the home we lived in at this time was very beautiful. There was an atrium in the entryway that had a huge bougainvillea plant growing in a large, decorative container. We actually had carpet on the floors and decent bathroom facilities. The woman who did the cooking was named Agatha, which to us in Spanish sounded like *aguila*, which in English means "eagle." As I recall, she was not nearly as good a cook as the one in El Salvador who was baptized into the Church.

This lady brought out some strange dishes, which I personally tried to stay away from. There was a wonderful Italian restaurant in Guatemala City by the name of Las Vegas. I can't remember if it was against the mission rules, but at least one night a week most of the elders and sisters working in the city would congregate at Las Vegas about 9 PM. Their best dish was lasagna, which I ordered every time we ate there. We were all working very hard, and so it didn't seem like a sin to meet and visit and see how everyone was getting along.

One night my companion and I missed the nine o'clock bus that would take us back to our home. Another one would not come along for approximately an hour, and we were unhappy about that. I leaned my back against a door adjacent to the bus stop, and as I did so it opened. I literally fell into a lady's living room. She screamed and was as astonished as we were over the situation. She soon was laughing and had a great personality and spirit about her. Before the next bus came, we taught her a discussion and she eventually was one of our baptisms in Guatemala City. I think the Lord wanted her in His Church.

The town of Coban was located high in the mountains of Guatemala. Although it was almost a twenty-hour bus ride from Guatemala City, it was part of my district. We flew there because of the treacherous mountainous roads one would have to traverse to visit this town. I went to Coban only once, and it was almost the last time I went anywhere. We flew in a plane that held, at most, ten people. It looked to me like it was held together by glue and bailing wire. I had little confidence that we would ever arrive at Coban but trusted that somehow the Lord would preserve our lives as we visited with the members and elders that were expecting us. To get to Coban the plane flew over some of the most rugged terrain in all of Guatemala. There were high mountains and deep canyons, and the plane was bucking and grinding with the constant change in the air currents. A little boy sitting across from me threw up, and I grabbed for the bag that was provided for such an emergency. Fortunately, I hung in there and was able to endure the flight, at least better than the little boy. As the plane descended, I could not see an airport and thought we were going in for a crash landing. However, it turned out that the airport and landing strip were nothing more than a long grassy meadow just outside of town.

I walked with quivering legs across the meadow to greet the missionaries who were working there. As I recall, I truly enjoyed being in this primitive outpost, where there was a small but thriving branch. The one memory I carry away from that visit was the beautiful white blouses worn by all the women in the town, which were beautifully embroidered with colorful flowers. How tragic that I did not keep a better account so I could have recalled more of the details of this trip. I can remember being very happy to be back in Guatemala City and did not repeat that adventure ever again. I suppose my next trip would have been the twenty-hour bus ride from Guatemala City to Coban because there was no way I would have ever flown in that little airplane up into those mountains again.

All of our baptisms in Guatemala City were performed in an outside baptismal font on the property that contained the mission home and the only chapel in the city. Almost every Saturday evening that I was in the city we had a large baptismal service. The nights were balmy, and the setting was idyllic. That immense Guatemalan moon would shine down through the large trees that surrounded the font, and in my mind I was at the Waters of Mormon with Alma and those who were entering into that sacred baptismal covenant described in Mosiah 18. At those baptismal services, I had feelings come to me from the Holy Ghost that left no doubt in my mind about the truthfulness of this work. I can remember on a number of occasions when our investigators were baptized, I would be so full of joy that I did not want anyone to speak to me out of fear that the feeling I was experiencing would go away. I can identify with Ammon and his being so overcome with joy that he fainted. I have experienced the same feelings of joy periodically during my life since the mission, and because of that my faith in Christ and in this latter-day work has become firm and, I hope, unshakable. The power of the Spirit communicating to our spirit is a more powerful witness than seeing something with our natural eye.

FEBRUARY 6, 1961

This has been a very interesting week, and also one that has helped me to have more faith. I would like to tell you about what happened to me this Friday. We were out in a little suburb to a home Primary, and we had to be to the chapel to interview people for the baptismal service on Saturday. They told me where there was a shortcut to the chapel from the suburbs and said I could walk faster than I could take a bus. I went by myself and I got lost. I ended up in an old field with some big bulls, and I'm kind of afraid of bulls anyway. By the time I could get to the main road it was really late, so I hopped a bus with the hope of getting there as quickly as possible. As I approached the chapel, I saw several people waiting out in front for me. So I jumped out of the bus, and ran in front of it. As I got out in front of the bus, I suddenly saw a car just zooming down the street, not 25 feet away. I was so scared I just froze, and luckily the driver had quick reflexes, because he braked and the car squealed to a stop a foot from my leg. I could feel it hit me, and then it didn't. It is as if some invisible hand came out of nowhere and stopped the car. Elder Wadsworth said he felt like someone kicked him in the stomach because he couldn't see how the car didn't hit me. I was white as a sheet for a while. The Lord protected me; that's all there is to it.

Everything is going just swell. We haven't been getting so many baptisms, but we have learned more than we did when we were baptizing so many. I have to spend more time working with my companion than I did before. Nevertheless, we baptized eight people last month and 22 the month before, which is good. The Lord blessed us with the baptisms, and He will bless us again when He sees fit to do so.

I now have been here 27 months, and before you know it, it will all be over down here. I have had such a successful, happy mission that I just could never thank the Lord enough for letting me serve Him.

Although I didn't mention it in the letter, poor Sister Hancock was standing on the other side of the road and witnessed me almost being struck by this car. She screamed and almost fainted. As a mother would do to a disobedient child, when she recovered her composure, she gave me an earful about being more careful.

MARCH 15, 1961

How is everything at home? It is great down here. We are going to baptize 250 people here in the city in just one month. My companion and I have to baptize 20 people in just one month. Last week we were blessed with 6, and the week before with 4, so you can see that we are still really going after it. Thirteen new elders just came from the states yesterday, all new, fresh, excited, and green. One of them is my companion. He is about six feet three inches tall and is a real wonderful fellow. We have been working on a training program for them so that they can learn Spanish and give all the lessons within the time of six weeks. If it works, it will be used throughout the world in all the Spanish-speaking missions. We hope it will work, and each Thursday we will be fasting down here for baptisms and for these new elders, so if you would like, once in a while you can help us out also by fasting and praying. We need your prayers; it helped us in December and it can also help us in the month starting March 15 and ending April 15.

MARCH 24, 1961

I have a lot of things to say today, a lot of questions so I'll start right off.

As you know I'll soon be winging back home, and I'd like to know a few things. First, have you ever thought of where you would like to meet me? Los Angeles, Salt Lake, or where? I'm going to leave this up to you, so you tell me where, and I'll see you there in May.

Yesterday President Hancock said he might like to keep me down here a few more weeks, and he told me to write home and ask you what you think about it. He might send me on a tour of the mission, presenting a new plan we have worked out. It's not sure yet, but he wanted me to write and ask what you think of it. Also, would you check with the army draft board and see what they say about it. I don't exactly want to get drafted and will undoubtedly get in for six months like everyone else. I would like to know this as soon as possible, and remember that it's not a sure deal yet. The most I would stay down would be two weeks longer. If I don't stay down, I will be leaving Guatemala the eighth of May on a jet headed for Los Angeles.

APRIL 4, 1961

Yesterday President Hancock definitely told me that I would be taking a tour of the mission, starting perhaps this coming week. I will be down here one week longer than my time. I should probably be coming home the 13th or 14th of May. As soon as I know the exact dates, I will let you know. Well, needless to say I'm just thrilled with this great opportunity and don't know why the Lord has blessed me so. I will first go to Costa Rica, Nicaragua, Honduras, El Salvador, and then home to Guatemala, and home to Nevada.

I will be working one day with each pair of missionaries in the mission and holding a workshop with each group in each country once a week.

It will take approximately one month to make the tour. What a chance to help the mission and serve the Lord. I am just writing this letter to let you know how happy I am.

P.S. I just received my schedule of the tour. I leave the 10th of April and get back to Guatemala the 20th of May, which is a Saturday.

# CHAPTER 13

# *Touring the Mission*

The companion President Hancock chose to send with me to tour the mission was a fairly new elder by the name of Dennis Morrill. I recall that he was very spiritually in tune and a great missionary. After his mission he received a law degree, and later was called to be president of the mission in Guatemala where my son John served. I believe he was John's president for the last six months of his mission. What a small world we live in!

San Jose, Costa Rica, April 16, 1961

Everything is just swell down here. Elder Morrill and I have been in Costa Rica for one week, and the tenth we will fly to Managua, Nicaragua. We work with each pair of elders one day, so that means a new town every day. We have a couple of air mattresses with us on which to sleep. So the sleeping is not so bad. Costa Rica is the most beautiful country of Central America and is called the Switzerland of the Americas. It is also the most Catholic country in Central America, and the work is kind of hard here. We have really been working hard, and I know that in spite of the Catholic Church, Costa Rica will go as well as Guatemala one day.

It is really a challenge working with every elder in the mission. I have to be at my best every day to be able to inspire and help the senior companions. The Lord has blessed me enormously, and I am thankful for my new calling.

We are fasting and praying for the mission every Sunday. I pray you can do the same. I leave Guatemala the 22nd of May on a jet. I'll fly from Los Angeles to Salt Lake and from there by bus or plane to Ely. The time flies when you are traveling. I have a lot to do, so I'll be seeing you. Take care of yourselves.

DANLI, HONDURAS, APRIL 27, 1961

I'm now in Danli, Honduras. It is an hour plane ride from Managua, Nicaragua, to the capital of Honduras, Tegucigalpa, and from Tegucigalpa to Danli it is five hours by Jeep right up in the mountains on a dirt road. This is the littlest town in the mission but also one of the most beautiful. Today we are going to go back to Tegucigalpa.

This has been the greatest experience of my life, and I will always be happy for this opportunity to serve my Heavenly Father. It is amazing to see the difference between these Central American countries. The people in each country are completely different from the people in the other countries. At this time we have traveled 2000 miles since the 10th of April. That is a lot of country to put behind you in not much time. It is really an education to get to see so many things and to get to work with so many different kinds of people.

We will be in Honduras until the 14th of May, at which time we will fly to San Salvador to work with the elders. We will be there until the 16th of May. The 16th we will go by bus to Guatemala to work in two border towns of El Salvador, arriving in the capital the 20th. The 22nd of May I'll leave Guatemala at 5 PM, fly to Los Angeles by jet, from Los Angeles to Salt Lake, and I guess from Salt Lake to Ely by plane. I'll do this, and if you want it any other way let me know soon, because they want to make my plane reservations any day now. I haven't heard from you since the 10th of April because our mail can't catch up with us. I imagine I will get your mail about the 14th of May, when I am in San Salvador.

The Lord has blessed Elder Morrill and me with the power to inspire the elders in each of the countries in which we have been. We have fasted and prayed and studied a great deal, and to this we contribute our success. We will continue to do this until they put me on the plane in Guatemala and ship me home. I love the work of the Lord and pray that someday I can help other people see that the only real joy in the world comes through unselfish dedication to the Lord's work. Peace is joy, and who is more happy and joyful than one who is doing the work of the Lord? The answer is obvious to anyone who has done church work of any kind; a missionary knows best of all.

Brigham Young said, "Many have such feelings that they are greater who are in the world preaching the gospel than those who remain here.

It is a grand mistake!" I agree with Brigham Young, for I know that you at home are just as important and greater than we are, and without your help this great work of love would not be able to go on.

May the Lord bless you always in all you do, and may he watch over you until we meet again I pray.

SANTA ANA, EL SALVADOR, MAY 15, 1961

This is the last letter I'll write you before I see you. I saw President Hancock in San Salvador yesterday, and he gave me some of my mail. I see that you plan on meeting me in Salt Lake City. I will be there the 23rd, Tuesday. However, when I reach Guatemala City the 20th I will find out the flight and time so you can be there to meet me. You should receive a telegram from me the 20th or 21st telling you the exact time. President Hancock was so thrilled with the work we have done through the mission that he wanted me to stay longer, but I know and he realizes also that the time has come to say good-bye. I have a great mission in life, and this is only the start. I don't know if I will ever be able to express to anyone how much joy you receive dedicating yourself to the Lord's work. I'll see you Tuesday in Salt Lake City.

I lament the fact that I did not keep a more detailed record of my tour of the mission. It was truly a magical time for Elder Morrill and me. We felt the Spirit so strongly as we taught the missionaries in each of the countries of Central America. I am not going to even attempt to re-create what happened during that month, but it was a special time in my mission and in my life. In appendix D is a letter from my former companion, Elder Farrer, with whom I worked in Chimaltenango when I got sick. He heard about my 1989 accident through an *Ensign* article, found my email address, and sent me the account from his journal of my visit to Danli, Honduras, as part of our tour of the mission.

*Elder Hal Farrer and Elder Rushton.*

I was most impressed with Costa Rica as being a clean and beautiful country. However, the missionary work has gone slower in Costa Rica than any other country in Central because the Spanish destroyed the Lamanite population through killing and disease. In San Jose, in particular, you have the feeling of being in a very European country. It is the most Catholic country in Central America, and although the Church has grown and there is a temple in Costa Rica, the work has been more difficult there. I remember working one day with the elders in the city of Cartago, which has a reputation of being the most Catholic city in the Western Hemisphere. No elders were assigned to that city, but we had gone to see just how difficult the work might be. We were welcomed into almost every home we went to, but the minute we brought up the subject of religion we were shown the door. I have no idea if there is a ward or branch in that city today. I would imagine there is, and I hope it is flourishing.

I also distinctly remember knocking on doors with another elder in a little town in Nicaragua. We knocked on one door, and a man came to the door and said he didn't want us around and to please leave. We went to the next door and knocked. Unbelievably it was the same house, and the man was just irate. We went to the next door, which turned out to be the same house, and the man came to the door with a large machete in his hand, cursing and waving it above his head. My companion and I decided it would be prudent to quickly leave that particular neighborhood.

Inevitably, the day finally came that I would leave Guatemala. I remember few vivid details of my departure, although I do know that some of the people we had baptized in the city came to see me off. President Hancock and I had a great love and respect for one another. He prepared a special letter of introduction to the First Presidency of the Church, wanting me to meet with them and explain what we were doing in our mission to train the missionaries and especially the new elders who were just arriving from the United States. In appendix E is a copy of the letter he wrote. I hate to admit that when I got to Salt Lake City I did not have enough courage to go to the Church Office Building and present my letter of introduction to somebody there. I felt that those great men would have little time to spend on the likes of me. It is hard to say what a great experience I may have passed up by not having enough faith or confidence in myself and the work I had done. For many years of my life, I think I missed other great opportunities because of a lack of self-confidence and a native shyness or bashfulness inherited from my mother. It is one thing to be humble and teachable, but it is an entirely different matter to lack the courage and confidence in one's self to reach out and take advantage of great opportunities that life may present. I am grateful to report that through the years I have almost conquered this problem.

# CHAPTER 14

# *Homecoming*

It was late afternoon when I left Guatemala City. I was alone. Having always had a companion at my side for two and a half years, I felt very strange. It was early evening when we landed at the Mexico City Airport. A taxi took me to the hotel that had been arranged for me. The room I had was the finest room I had slept in since I had left the United States. The bed was so soft compared to what I was accustomed to that I spent the night sleeping on the floor next to the bed. Feeling lonely, I noticed when we had arrived at the hotel that there was a large movie theater just a few buildings away from where I was staying. I decided I would go to the movies to use up some of the time I had on my hands. The movie that was playing was *Elmer Gantry,* starring Burt Lancaster. It was in English with the subtitles in Spanish, and I enjoyed it and still do to this day. Movie theaters in Latin America in those days were always the most beautiful and lavish buildings in town. Our Lamanite brothers and sisters love to go to the movies and, I believe, escape from the harsh realities of their day-to-day fight for survival. I left the theater and hurried back to my room but slept fitfully, not wanting to oversleep and miss my flight to Los Angeles and then to Salt Lake City. I hailed a taxi early that morning and was finally at peace as I settled myself into my seat on the plane and enjoyed the flight to Los Angeles. After a brief layover in Los Angeles I was on my way to Salt Lake City.

It is still vividly etched into my mind how the Salt Lake Valley looked to me as we flew into the airport from Los Angeles. The Wasatch Mountains were still covered with snow because it was early in the spring, but compared to the lush jungles and landscapes of Central America, it truly looked like a desert. Somehow my arrival time had been given incorrectly to my family, and nobody was at the airport when I descended from the airplane in all my post-missionary glory. I called my brother Darrel, who was not at home, but his wife, Leann, drove to the airport to pick me up. It was good to see her, and soon Darrel came home. Within a few hours, we drove back to the airport to meet my mom and dad and brother, Kim. They were all anxiously awaiting the arrival of the airplane and were so surprised when I walked up behind them and said hello. It was a great reunion, and I basked in the joy of being reunited with my family once again.

The next day my parents bought me a new suit at ZCMI because the suit I came home in was one big rag. Later that afternoon we drove to Ely, Nevada, and when I finally walked into my boyhood home I knew that my mission was indeed over. I had a difficult time adjusting both physically and emotionally to life after my mission. Everything seemed so unimportant compared to the fight to win the souls of my Lamanite brothers and sisters. However, eventually life went on as it always does, and I began to anticipate the new challenges that awaited me now that I had concluded my call to serve.

# EPILOGUE

My mission was the defining experience of my life. Because of it, I would never be the same person again. I entered the mission field as a naïve boy from a little mining town in Nevada. I didn't know the scriptures, the gospel, or the Lord. Thankfully, though, I did have sufficient faith to accept the call. In the mission field, my faith in Heavenly Father and Jesus Christ began to grow and deepen. I returned home with an expanded vision of life and its possibilities as well as the knowledge that I was capable of doing things I had previously thought impossible. Things that seemed important before, such as pursuing a career in music, now seemed trivial and unimportant. Much to the consternation of my mother after my mission, I never played the clarinet again and only played the piano for the joy it brought to me and others.

Because of my mission I pursued a career as a seminary and institute teacher. I brought home with me such a desire to search the scriptures and teach others, especially the youth, that no other career could have satisfied that fire that continues to burn in my soul. Without my mission experience, I doubt I would ever have developed the strength spiritually and emotionally to deal with living as a quadriplegic for so many years.

Recently my son John's former mission president, Gilberto Cerda, who is one of the five stake presidents of the Spanish-speaking stakes in Southern California, asked me to speak in Spanish to a five-stake gathering of single adults. I hesitated to do so, but recalling my mission and the debt of gratitude I owe to the people of Central America, I consented. I agonized for the first few days as I prepared to speak in Spanish in public, which I had not done for a number of years, and then a wonderful thing happened. The Spanish words I needed came up from deep in my subconscious, and with some help from a Hispanic lady who lives in our neighborhood, I was able to get my talk into my mind and into my heart in Spanish. The night of the gathering I was able to speak fluently for an hour and was transported back in time to the streets and chapels of my mission. I felt so comfortable with my Lamanite brothers and sisters and knew that I was connecting with them as I had as a young missionary.

As Jo Anne and I left the chapel that night with President Cerda, I said to him, "President, why is it that I relate so well to these people and love them so much?"

He simply said, "It is because you lost your *gringo* heart in Guatemala and have been one of us ever since." I think he was right!

# APPENDIX A

## *Early Missionary Experiences in Patzicia, Guatemala, as Told by Berkley Arnold Spencer*

The town of Patzicia in the district of Chimaltenango, Guatemala, was opened to missionary work on December 15, 1956. Elder Phil Leigh, counselor in the Central American Mission presidency accompanied Elder Nello Earl Deschamps, senior companion, and Elder Berkley Arnold Spencer to Patzicia to begin the work of teaching the gospel of Christ to the people.

To most effectively begin the work in Patzicia, it was decided that first efforts would be among the Ladino people (of mixed Indian and Spanish blood) who spoke both Spanish and Cakchiquel. It was reasoned that good converts from among the Ladinos could then gradually help expand the missionary efforts among the Cakchiquel Indians. Consequently, the first three weeks were spent in visiting evangelical churches, municipal authorities, and prominent citizens of the community, all of whom were Ladino.

Unknown at that time to us was the fact that Patzicia had been the site about twelve years earlier of a political conflict during the transition between the presidency of Ponce and Juan Jose Arevalo, which led to the massacre of approximately 300 Cakchiquel men, women, and children. Over a year after Patzicia had been opened, President Edgar LeRoy Wagner related the circumstances under which the decision was made to send missionaries to Patzicia. He indicated that every time he drove through Patzicia as he traveled between Guatemala City and the communities in the western highlands he felt he should send missionaries there. As he inquired of local members in Guatemala City about Patzicia, he was told of the massacre and was warned that if he sent missionaries they would be returned to him in caskets. The people, he was told, were very bad.

During the first three weeks in Patzicia, we encountered a great deal of interest in our message. Discussions were many and prospects for converts seemed very good. Toward the end of the second week of January, however, the first indications of serious opposition began to be manifest. We began to hear that people were saying evil things about us; even some of those who had expressed great interest in the gospel were said to be spreading evil rumors.

On January 21, 1957, the opposition came to a head in the following event as described in my journal:

> As Elder Deschamps and I were walking one of the upper streets to a visit, some little kids ran up to us and told us that a man wanted to talk to us at the *jusgado* (courthouse). We told them to wait a minute, but they said it was the *alcalde* (mayor), so we decided we had better comply. As we were walking back, we noticed they were giggling a little, so we kept asking them if they were telling the truth. They swore they were, so we kept going.
>
> I noticed as we came into view of the jusgado, there was quite a group of people standing around looking and another group in the building. As we walked across the plaza, the people all focused on us, and we were immediately the center of attention. As we walked into the building, I felt a bit uneasy but was determined that as ambassadors of the Lord we would represent Him with every dignity and power which was rightfully ours. Once inside the entrance, a lady met us, saying that we were not wanted inside but that the persons who wanted to talk to us were outside waiting. She was very anxious for us not to see the *alcalde*, so we went right on into the secretary's office.
>
> While we were inside, the *alcalde* in his adjacent office was talking to a large group of Indian people. As we stood waiting, the owner of the pharmacy, who is very Catholic, told us (upon being asked) that some people were trying to make a complaint against us. He also assured us that they had no right under the constitution to make any complaint or demonstration. As we were waiting, I was certainly praying to my Father in Heaven, and I'm sure Elder Deschamps was doing the same. Finally the crowd in the mayor's office was dismissed, and we were ushered in and asked to take a seat.
>
> The mayor, Jorge Vela, the pharmacy man, and another man were in the office. The mayor told us that some people were trying to circulate

> a complaint saying that we were entering the houses and leaving our message by force. We assured him that we were only going from house to house leaving our message with those who would let us in. He then told us that we had every right under the constitution and that he had called the governor just to make sure. I then told him that he and the rest there should hear our message to know exactly what it is so that they could inform the people if we were preaching something contrary. We finally left the office with the assurance that we were perfectly upheld by the constitution.
>
> When we got outside, we were met by a group of Catholic women and men who told us that there were some men who wanted to talk to us up at the Catholic church. We told them we were very sorry but we had some visits to attend. They started trying to convince us to come up and talk for five minutes. Elder Deschamps was doing the talking and told them we couldn't. Finally when they saw we weren't, they tried to get us to leave town. They said we were leading away the ignorant people and were causing a division in the *pueblo* (town).
>
> We finally just started to walk off, but there was by that time a great crowd of people around us. Strangely enough, as we walked away the crowd just opened up, and I noticed some men whom I hadn't seen before were clearing the path in front of us. Also, amazingly, as we walked away not one word of jeering or spite was said by anyone. . . .
>
> When we got home, Elis Salazar came and told us that he heard say that the chapel was filled with Indians with sticks, machetes, etc. He also said that from one of the Post Office men he had learned that the governor in Chimaltenango told the *alcalde* to "disperse that crowd, or he would come and do it with gunshots."

During the month of February, we continued to work with the Ladinos but had little success except with two families, the Teodoro Tecun family, and the family of Doña Seferina de la Cruz. As it became apparent that most of the Ladinos had little sincere interest in the Church, we began to consider changing our strategy by working directly with the Indian people.

Two major challenges loomed large. The first was that we could not find a suitable house to rent for a chapel. Those who had a suitable house would not rent to the Mormons. The second challenge was that the Indian people were always out working in the fields. It was extremely difficult to find the Indian men home on a consistent basis. So we decided to adjust our schedule to fit that of the people. We started getting up at 5:30 AM, going out at 6:00 AM, returning to eat breakfast at 9:00 AM, going out again at 11:00 AM until 2:00 PM, returning for lunch and study until 5:00 PM, then returning home for supper at 9:00 PM. This schedule enabled us to meet with the men before they went to the fields, or at other times when some were home.

On March 15, 1957, we visited a small village, La Canoa, forming one of the *aldeas* (hamlets) of Patzicia. Several good families were found. By the end of March, visits with the Indian people had grown both in number and in quality, we had discovered the importance of committing people to prepare for baptism early in the discussions, and on March 30 the first baptisms were held. Brother Teodoro Tecun; his wife, Juana Velasquez de Tecun; their son, Benigno; and Doña Seferina de la Cruz were the first members in Patzicia.

Two good Indian families who were found in April as a result of our new schedule were those of Daniel Mich and Luis Alonzo.

On several occasions, between 8:00 AM and 5:00 PM, the elders had passed by the fenced lot where Daniel Mich and his family lived. Each time as they knocked at the gate and asked if the man of the house was there, a kindly little Cakchiquel woman a little over four feet tall, dressed in her typical dress, would sweep her arm toward the mountain and say, "*Ixpepa cuyu*" (He has gone to the mountain). One morning soon after changing our schedule, we knocked at the same gate at 6:00 AM. This time an Indian man answered the door and with a broad smile asked us to come in and sit down in the corn storage shed. He indicated he would soon be off to the mountain to weed his corn crop but said he had been hopeful for a visit and invited us to share our message.

What started out to be a short visit turned into an hour-long discussion. He told us he had been rejected by the evangelical churches because he had been involved in the political uprising of 1944 and had spent eight years in prison. He asked if the Mormon Church would hold that against him. When we talked about the principle of repentance, the mercy of Jesus Christ, and the righteous judgment of God, he was touched and agreed to visit again on another occasion. One visit led to another, and on June 26, 1958, at 6:15 AM, Daniel Mich, Sister Cruz de Mich and their youngest son, Clemente, were baptized.

As we got to know the Mich family better, it became clear that the Lord had prepared Daniel to be an instrument in His hands to help establish the Church in Patzicia. Through Daniel, many members of his extended family began to receive the gospel message. It is estimated that over 200 friends and relatives eventually joined the Church as a direct consequence of his testimony.

On a later occasion, Daniel shared with us how he felt the Lord had protected him and his brothers during the massacre of 1944. He indicated that because he had been involved in the political activities leading up to that event, he and his family were prime candidates for reprisal by the Ladinos. Consequently he and his brothers fled to the mountains to the south of Patzicia. The following is an entry from my journal:

> They were hiding in the hills, and each had been stationed at a different point keeping watch. Daniel fell asleep because the sun was so warm and he had been so cold and so tired during the night of their fleeing Patzicia. He had a vision like a dream. Two men dressed in white robes with long hair came to him and said, "Wake up, Daniel; here come the wolves." "Daniel, wake up; the wolves are coming." When he opened his eyes, he could hear the barking of dogs in the distance. He woke up his brothers, and they began to flee up the mountain, and as they reached a ridge they looked back and saw about 40 armed men.
>
> He told us how they were traveling to Guatemala City in the back of a truck when they were stopped at a village. But the Lord protected them by hiding them. Finally, worried about his family, he went back to Patzicia, and there a bunch of Ladinos grabbed him, mistreated him, and accused him of killing three people. He was tried and sentenced to be shot, but while awaiting execution his sentence was changed to 30 years in prison. After eight years, President Juan Jose Arevalo finally pardoned him.

# APPENDIX B

## *Letter from Rosita Alvarado to Jack Rushton*

August 7, 1994, Guatemala

My beloved Brother Rushton:

You cannot imagine the joy I feel as I write this letter. I am overwhelmed with happiness to have this opportunity. You are a wonderful son of God.

Tears rolled out of my eyes because of the gratitude and joy I feel to know that you, one day, fulfilled the commandment of the Lord and served a full-time mission. The Lord called you to serve in Guatemala, and the Spirit prompted you to knock on the door of a modest home where a family was about to be dissolved.

It has been 34 years since that day. And even though I was only a little girl, I have never forgotten how gently you picked me up and carried me to Church. You and your companion were so kind to me.

Brother Rushton, I want you to know that we have always remembered you. My mom will be forever grateful to God and to you and your companion for bringing the gospel of Jesus Christ to our home.

Back then we were only four children. My parents had four more, and now we are eight. I want to share with you the happiness and some of the blessings we have enjoyed during these 34 years. Five of us have served full-time missions; four of us were called to serve in the Guatemala Quezaltenango Mission. My youngest brother finished his mission 15 months ago, he served in Panamá, and at the end of his mission he was serving as an assistant to the president. Six of us have been married and sealed in the temple of the Lord. We all have callings. Two of my brothers are counselors in the stake presidency, one in Guatemala and the other in California. My dad is a counselor in our ward. My mom is the ward chorister and the visiting teacher coordinator. My sister, who lives in Seattle, Washington, married a returned missionary, and they have been called to preside over a small Spanish-speaking branch. Her husband was born here and served his Mission in Chile.

My Brother Rushton, I share these blessings with you in humility, hoping that you can feel the joy of knowing of the many blessings that one of the families that you converted into the gospel has received.

Since I came back from my mission, the Lord has given me the opportunity to serve him in different callings. Currently I serve as a temple worker and as the young women's president of my ward.

When your son, Elder Rushton, came to our area, my mom recognized him right away. She says that he looks just like you. The Lord gave us the blessing to meet one of your children as he serves as his father did. My beloved Brother Rushton, I hope everything is well with you, and I also hope that you can feel joy in knowing that one of your sons is coming home from the mission field.

Thank you for teaching your children how to be faithful children of God. We know you have taught them well because we see how special your son is as a missionary. Please tell your wife and children to be proud of you and your son.

May our sweet Heavenly Father bless you. Thank you so much. Thank you for bringing the gospel of Jesus Christ to our home 34 years ago.

With love,<br>
Sister Rosita Alvarado

# APPENDIX C

## *Letter from Eduardo Alvarado to Jack Rushton*

February 28, 1993

Brother Jack Rushton:

It gives me great joy to have the opportunity to write to you. As I do it, I hope everything is well with you.

Do you know who I am? My name is Eduardo Alvarado. I am 33 years old. I am the fourth of eight children. My mom's name is Maria Gloria Oseida Montenegro, and my dad's name is José Guillermo Alvarado Avila. You baptized my mom on November 26, 1960. My dad was baptized in March 1961.

In my heart, I had always had a feeling of gratitude toward those missionaries that reached out to my parents. I believe your companion's last name was Jensen.

I met your son, Elder Rushton, in Ciudad Real. I was thrilled to know that you are alive and that I will finally have the chance to thank you for all that you did for my parents. My mom tells me that you used to carry me to church. I do not remember. Do you? I hope you do.

At the time of my parent's baptism, we lived in Zona 12, Avenida Petapa. In 1963 we moved to Ciudad Real. My parents stopped going to church for about five years because of some bad experiences we had due to our poverty. But we all came back to Church in 1971.

Now we are eight children. Five of us have served full-time missions. My youngest brother is currently serving in Panamá; he will be home in April. I was the first one to serve in the Guatemala

*Eduardo Alvarado and family, Guatemala City.*

Quezaltenango Mission. I served among the K'ekch'i people and learned their language from January 29, 1979, to January 29, 1981. I was sealed in the Mexico City Temple on May 15, 1984. I have three beautiful daughters: Sarita, Damaris, and Andrea. I am currently serving as the bishop of the Barrio Union, here in Villa Nueva. I have a small business, a metal vise shop I opened last August.

My Heavenly Father has blessed me so much. I am so happy. I am overwhelmed at the many blessings I have received throughout my life.

Brother Rushton, I want to thank you. Thank you for finding my parents when they needed more. Back then they were about to separate, but because of the gospel they are still together and happy. Now they are 62 and 58 years old. We have been sealed as a family in the Arizona Temple in December 1981. We would have been sealed before, but we didn't have enough money. The earthquake of 1976 affected our family greatly; besides, we always "enjoy" much poverty. Now we have enough money for our needs.

Three of my brothers live in the United States (California, Salt Lake, and Washington); one is serving a mission in Panamá. By the way, we are six brothers and two sisters. You only met Able, German, Rosita, and me. Rosita was three years old when you met her. She was suffering from polio, which affected her body and never developed normally, but she still served a mission from 1980 to June 1981.

I have almost put you up to date on what has happened with my family. In sharing this with you my only intention is to show you the fruits of your labor. We are not perfect, but we strive to live the gospel. I know the honor and glory go to our Heavenly Father, but as His instruments, isn't it nice to see what has happened in the lives of the people you baptized 33 years ago?

I have a strong testimony of the gospel. I follow Jesus Christ. I know He lives and loves us. Someday we will see each other again. Brother Rushton, I appreciate you. Please share this letter with your wife.

May you always be happy.

Sincerely,
Eduardo Alvarado

# APPENDIX D

## *Letter from Hal Farrer to Jack Rushton*

May 6, 1994

Dear Jack,

In view of all the worthy acclaim and excitement likely resulting from the recent writeup about you in the April 1994 *Ensign* magazine, can you handle one more fan letter—from an old mission field companion who was your junior in the Chimaltenango district of Guatemala, back in 1960?

I was about one-third of the way through reading the article before I suddenly realized they were talking about my former compañero and district president up in the Indian country of Chimaltenango, Patzicia, Patzun and Tecpan, some 34 years ago—whom we called "the Chief" and who taught us a great deal about missionary work, and about playing the piano!

It had been many years since I had heard anything from or about you, and was totally unaware of your tragic 1989 accident while body-surfing—and I have difficulty expressing how shocked and saddened I was to read of it, particularly when remembering what an active and involved missionary you were. Always busy and "about our Father's business"—and it sounds like you've been busy on the Lord's errand ever since!

I remember the last time I saw you in the mission field—I was laboring in the small town of Danli, Honduras, when you toured the mission with a new proselyting program for the elders, just before you came home. I looked up my old mission journal entry for that day:

"25 April '61: Quite a surprise today—we had two visiting elders today, Dennis Morrill, and Jack Louis Rushton Jr.! The 'Chief' after all this time! Gee, I was sure glad to see him. He's touring the mission before he goes home, with a new program from the workshop in Guatemala. We talked over old times during supper, and we went to the D&C study class at the chapel, during which the Chief played a solo, 'The Dream of Olwen.' I'm going to get a record of that when I get home. After meeting I showed him all the pictures I took in Chimaltenango after he left. We turned in at 10 PM, me on the Chief's air mattress and he in my bed."

Hal Farrer

# APPENDIX E

## *Letter from Victor C. Hancock to Henry D. Moyle*

May 22, 1961

The First Presidency
47 East South Temple
Salt Lake City, Utah

Attention: President Henry D. Moyle

Dear President Moyle:

The Central American Mission has just finished another course in the training program for the new missionaries. Thank you very much for completing the quota of 150 full-time missionaries which you promised us.

Elder Jack Rushton was one of the two who has been guiding this program from the beginning. As you recall, this training program brought into the mission headquarters the leading elders of the mission. While these elders were training the new missionaries, they held workshops periodically. These workshops have also proved to be beneficial to the whole mission, for some of these leaders are now going out in the various districts upgrading the work and holding workshops with the missionaries.

With this in mind, Elder Rushton went to Costa Rica, trained another outstanding elder, and came up through the mission with him, working individually with the missionaries and then holding workshops. This has been the best thing that has happened in this mission since we came down.

I should like to recommend him to you as one of the outstanding elders in training missionaries and in conducting workshops in the mission field. I wish Elder Rushton could be with me to work longer, but the time has come to release him.

Should you be interested at this time to hear more about the training program, perhaps Elder Rushton could explain the details to you.

Sincerely yours,

Victor C. Hancock
Mission President

# ABOUT THE AUTHOR

Jack Rushton was born and raised in White Pine County, Nevada. He attended Brigham Young University, where he received his bachelor's degree and a master's degree in counseling and guidance. He also received a doctor of education degree from USC. He was actively involved in religious education, both as a teacher and an administrator for twenty-five years.

In August of 1989, he suffered a severe accident while swimming in the ocean. It left him paralyzed from the neck down and on life support. Jack and his wife, Jo Anne, are the parents of six children and have sixteen grandchildren. They have lived in Tustin, California, since 1974.

Since his accident, Jack has been able to continue to teach, counsel, and deliver motivational talks to a variety of adult and youth audiences. Although his life is very different from what it once was, he continues to find joy and fulfillment in it and can often be heard to say, "It's good to be alive!"

0 26575 51180 2